WILLIAM SHAKESPEARE
MACBETH

The First Folio

Illustrated by Von

OVAL PROJECTS LIMITED · SIDGWICK & JACKSON LIMITED

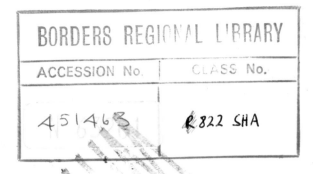
Produced by Oval Projects Limited,
335 Kennington Road, London SE11 4QE

British Library Cataloguing in Publication Data
Shakespeare, William
    Macbeth.–(Cartoon Shakespeare)
    1. Shakespeare, William. Macbeth–Pictorial works
    I. Title   II. Tauté, Anne
    III. Von   IV. Series
    822.3'3   PR2823

ISBN 0 283 98888 6 hardcover
ISBN 0 283 98906 8 softcover

Edited by Anne Tauté
Jacket design by Jim Wire, Charing, Kent
Lettering by Brian Robins, Nunhead, London SE15
Origination by Colourscan Co Pte Ltd, Singapore
Printed by Mandarin Offset (HK) Ltd, Hong Kong

Distributed by Sidgwick & Jackson Limited,
1 Tavistock Chambers, Bloomsbury Way,
London WC1A 2SG

THE PLOT

Macbeth and **Banquo,** generals of **King Duncan's** army, have defeated a rebellion and repulsed a Norwegian invasion. Going home they are stopped by three wild witches who tell Macbeth he will be thane of Cawdor and King of Scotland. But Banquo's children will be future kings. As they vanish in the mist, the first prophecy comes true. Inspired by their words Macbeth considers murder. **Lady Macbeth** sharpens his resolve, and he stabs Duncan to death.

The crown is now his, but fear and suspicion shadow him. Macbeth cannot forget the prediction made to Banquo. He hires assassins to kill his friend, but Banquo's dreadful ghost comes back to haunt him. Macbeth seeks out the witches and is warned against **Macduff,** the thane of Fife, but told no harm can come to him till someone not 'of woman born' appears, and Birnam forest moves.

Macbeth is told Macduff has fled to England to join forces with **Malcolm,** the son of murdered Duncan. Enraged he has Macduff's wife and family slaughtered. Lady Macbeth demented by so much bloodshed, starts sleepwalking.

Macbeth prepares to defend his fortress and is shaken to hear that Birnam wood is moving. Hidden by branches hacked from the forest Malcolm and Macduff's army overruns the castle. Macbeth resists attack, confident no man can kill him. But Macduff reveals he was cut from the womb and so not 'born' of woman. They fight. Macbeth is slain. Malcolm is at last made King.

Written in 1606, on the wave of support and loyalty to King James VI & I after the Gunpowder Plot attempt on his life, Shakespeare was deliberately indulging his monarch's known obsessions with Scottish history, ancestry, and witchcraft. Murder, treason, suspicion, witches, were the topics of the day, and public interest was particularly caught by the case of a priest who, having been accused of lying at his trial, maintained that he was not lying, but merely concealing the truth with double meaning . . .

ACT 1, SCENE 1

WHEN SHALL WE THREE MEET AGAIN ?
IN THUNDER, LIGHTNING, OR IN RAIN ?

WHEN THE HURLY-BURLY'S DONE,
WHEN THE BATTLE'S LOST AND WON.

THAT WILL BE ERE THE SET OF SUN.

WHERE THE PLACE ?

UPON THE HEATH.

THERE TO MEET WITH MACBETH.

I COME, GREY-MALKIN !

PADDOCK CALLS.

ANON !

FAIR IS FOUL, AND FOUL IS FAIR : HOVER THROUGH THE FOG AND FILTHY AIR.

WHAT BLOODY MAN IS THAT?
HE CAN REPORT, AS SEEMETH BY HIS PLIGHT,
OF THE REVOLT THE NEWEST STATE.

THIS IS THE SERGEANT, WHO
LIKE A GOOD AND HARDY SOLDIER
FOUGHT 'GAINST MY CAPTIVITY.
HAIL, BRAVE FRIEND! SAY TO THE KING
THE KNOWLEDGE OF THE BROIL
AS THOU DIDST LEAVE IT.

DOUBTFUL IT STOOD,
AS TWO SPENT SWIMMERS,
THAT DO CLING TOGETHER
AND CHOKE THEIR ART. THE
MERCILESS MACDONWALD—
WORTHY TO BE A REBEL,
FOR TO THAT THE
MULTIPLYING VILLAINIES
OF NATURE DO SWARM
UPON HIM—

FROM THE WESTERN ISLES
OF KERNS AND GALLOWGLASSES IS SUPPLIED;
AND FORTUNE, ON HIS DAMNÈD QUARREL
SMILING, SHOWED LIKE A REBEL'S WHORE:
BUT ALL'S TOO WEAK:

FOR BRAVE MACBETH — WELL HE DESERVES THAT NAME —
DISDAINING FORTUNE, WITH HIS BRANDISHED STEEL,
WHICH SMOKED WITH BLOODY EXECUTION,
LIKE VALOUR'S MINION CARVÈD OUT HIS PASSAGE,

TILL HE FACED
THE SLAVE;
WHICH NE'ER SHOOK HANDS,
NOR BADE FAREWELL
TO HIM,

TILL HE UNSEAMED HIM
FROM THE NAVE TO THE
CHOPS, AND FIXED HIS
HEAD UPON OUR BATTLEMENTS.

3

O VALIANT COUSIN! WORTHY GENTLEMAN!

AS WHENCE THE SUN 'GINS HIS REFLECTION SHIPWRACKING STORMS AND DIREFUL THUNDERS BREAK, SO FROM THAT SPRING WHENCE COMFORT SEEMED TO COME, DISCOMFORT SWELLS.

MARK, KING OF SCOTLAND, MARK: NO SOONER JUSTICE HAD WITH VALOUR ARMED, COMPELLED THESE SKIPPING KERNS TO TRUST

THEIR HEELS, BUT THE NORWEYAN LORD, SURVEYING VANTAGE, WITH FURBISHED ARMS AND NEW SUPPLIES OF MEN, BEGAN A FRESH ASSAULT.

DISMAYED NOT THIS OUR CAPTAINS, MACBETH AND BANQUO?

YES; AS SPARROWS, EAGLES, OR THE HARE, THE LION. IF I SAY SOOTH, I MUST REPORT THEY WERE AS CANNONS OVERCHARGED WITH DOUBLE CRACKS; SO THEY DOUBLY REDOUBLED STROKES UPON THE FOE: EXCEPT THEY MEANT TO BATHE IN REEKING WOUNDS, OR MEMORIZE ANOTHER GOLGOTHA, I CANNOT TELL:

BUT I AM FAINT, MY GASHES CRY FOR HELP.

SO WELL THY WORDS BECOME THEE AS THY WOUNDS; THEY SMACK OF HONOUR BOTH. GO GET HIM SURGEONS.

WHO COMES HERE?

THE WORTHY THANE OF ROSS.

WHAT A HASTE LOOKS THROUGH HIS EYES! SO SHOULD HE LOOK THAT SEEMS TO SPEAK THINGS STRANGE.

GOD SAVE THE KING!

WHENCE CAM'ST THOU, WORTHY THANE?

FROM FIFE, GREAT KING,

WHERE THE NORWEYAN BANNERS FLOUT THE SKY AND FAN OUR PEOPLE COLD.

NORWAY HIMSELF, WITH TERRIBLE NUMBERS, ASSISTED BY THAT MOST DISLOYAL TRAITOR, THE THANE OF CAWDOR, BEGAN A DISMAL CONFLICT;

TILL THAT BELLONA'S BRIDEGROOM, LAPPED IN PROOF, CONFRONTED HIM WITH SELF-COMPARISONS,

POINT AGAINST POINT, REBELLIOUS ARM 'GAINST ARM, CURBING HIS LAVISH SPIRIT: AND, TO CONCLUDE, THE VICTORY FELL ON US.

GREAT HAPPINESS!

THAT NOW SWENO, THE NORWAYS' KING, CRAVES COMPOSITION; NOR WOULD WE DEIGN HIM BURIAL OF HIS MEN TILL HE DISBURSÈD, AT SAINT COLME'S INCH, TEN THOUSAND DOLLARS TO OUR GENERAL USE.

NO MORE THAT THANE OF CAWDOR SHALL DECEIVE OUR BOSOM INTEREST. GO PRONOUNCE HIS PRESENT DEATH, AND WITH HIS FORMER TITLE GREET MACBETH.

I'LL SEE IT DONE.

WHAT HE HATH LOST, NOBLE MACBETH HATH WON.

ACT I SCENE III

WHERE HAST THOU BEEN, SISTER?

KILLING SWINE.

SISTER, WHERE THOU?

I'LL GIVE THEE A WIND.

AND I ANOTHER.

TH'ART KIND.

A SAILOR'S WIFE HAD CHESTNUTS IN HER LAP, AND MUNCHED, AND MUNCHED, AND MUNCHED: 'GIVE ME,' QUOTH I. 'AROINT THEE, WITCH!' THE RUMP-FED RONYON CRIES. HER HUSBAND'S TO ALEPPO GONE, MASTER O'THE TIGER: BUT IN A SIEVE I'LL THITHER SAIL, AND LIKE A RAT WITHOUT A TAIL, I'LL DO, I'LL DO, AND I'LL DO.

I MYSELF HAVE ALL THE OTHER; AND THE VERY PORTS THEY BLOW, ALL THE QUARTERS THAT THEY KNOW I'THE SHIPMAN'S CARD. I'LL DRAIN HIM DRY AS HAY: SLEEP SHALL NEITHER NIGHT NOR DAY HANG UPON HIS PENTHOUSE LID; HE SHALL LIVE A MAN FORBID. WEARY SEV'NIGHTS NINE TIMES NINE SHALL HE DWINDLE, PEAK AND PINE: THOUGH HIS BARK CANNOT BE LOST, YET IT SHALL BE TEMPEST-TOSSED. LOOK WHAT I HAVE!

SHOW ME, SHOW ME!

HERE I HAVE A PILOT'S THUMB, WRACKED AS HOMEWARD HE DID COME.

A DRUM! A DRUM! MACBETH DOTH COME.

THE WEIRD SISTERS, HAND IN HAND, POSTERS OF THE SEA AND LAND, THUS DO GO, ABOUT, ABOUT: THRICE TO THINE, AND THRICE TO MINE, AND THRICE AGAIN, TO MAKE UP NINE. PEACE! THE CHARM'S WOUND UP.

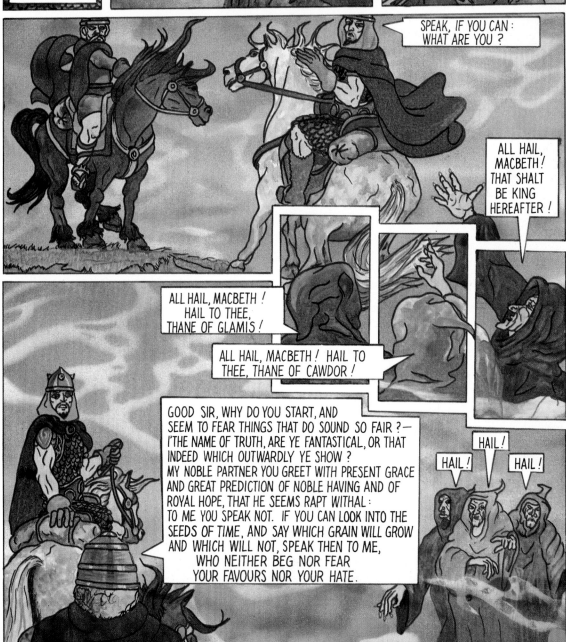

ENTER MACBETH AND BANQUO.

SO FOUL AND FAIR A DAY I HAVE NOT SEEN.

HOW FAR IS'T CALLED TO FORRES? WHAT ARE THESE, SO WITHERED AND SO WILD IN THEIR ATTIRE, THAT LOOK NOT LIKE THE INHABITANTS O'THE EARTH, AND YET ARE ON'T?

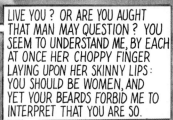

LIVE YOU? OR ARE YOU AUGHT THAT MAN MAY QUESTION? YOU SEEM TO UNDERSTAND ME, BY EACH AT ONCE HER CHOPPY FINGER LAYING UPON HER SKINNY LIPS: YOU SHOULD BE WOMEN, AND YET YOUR BEARDS FORBID ME TO INTERPRET THAT YOU ARE SO.

SPEAK, IF YOU CAN: WHAT ARE YOU?

ALL HAIL, MACBETH! THAT SHALT BE KING HEREAFTER!

ALL HAIL, MACBETH! HAIL TO THEE, THANE OF GLAMIS!

ALL HAIL, MACBETH! HAIL TO THEE, THANE OF CAWDOR!

GOOD SIR, WHY DO YOU START, AND SEEM TO FEAR THINGS THAT DO SOUND SO FAIR?— I'THE NAME OF TRUTH, ARE YE FANTASTICAL, OR THAT INDEED WHICH OUTWARDLY YE SHOW? MY NOBLE PARTNER YOU GREET WITH PRESENT GRACE AND GREAT PREDICTION OF NOBLE HAVING AND OF ROYAL HOPE, THAT HE SEEMS RAPT WITHAL: TO ME YOU SPEAK NOT. IF YOU CAN LOOK INTO THE SEEDS OF TIME, AND SAY WHICH GRAIN WILL GROW AND WHICH WILL NOT, SPEAK THEN TO ME, WHO NEITHER BEG NOR FEAR YOUR FAVOURS NOR YOUR HATE.

HAIL!

HAIL!

HAIL!

LESSER THAN MACBETH,
AND GREATER.

NOT SO HAPPY,
YET MUCH HAPPIER.

THOU SHALT GET KINGS,
THOUGH THOU BE NONE:
SO ALL HAIL,
MACBETH AND BANQUO!

BANQUO AND MACBETH, ALL HAIL!

STAY, YOU IMPERFECT SPEAKERS, TELL ME MORE.
BY SINEL'S DEATH I KNOW I AM THANE OF GLAMIS,
BUT HOW OF CAWDOR? THE THANE OF CAWDOR LIVES,
A PROSPEROUS GENTLEMAN; AND TO BE KING
STANDS NOT WITHIN THE PROSPECT OF BELIEF,
NO MORE THAN TO BE CAWDOR. SAY FROM WHENCE
YOU OWE THIS STRANGE INTELLIGENCE? OR WHY
UPON THIS BLASTED HEATH YOU STOP OUR WAY
WITH SUCH PROPHETIC GREETING?
SPEAK, I CHARGE YOU.

THE EARTH HATH BUBBLES,
AS THE WATER HAS,
AND THESE ARE OF THEM.
WHITHER ARE THEY VANISHED?

INTO THE AIR; AND WHAT SEEMED CORPORAL,
MELTED, AS BREATH INTO THE WIND.
WOULD THEY HAD STAYED!

WERE SUCH THINGS HERE AS WE DO SPEAK ABOUT?
OR HAVE WE EATEN ON THE INSANE ROOT
THAT TAKES THE REASON PRISONER?

YOUR CHILDREN
SHALL BE KINGS.

YOU SHALL BE KING.

AND THANE OF CAWDOR TOO:
WENT IT NOT SO?

TO THE SELFSAME TUNE AND WORDS.

ENTER ROSS AND ANGUS.

WHO'S HERE?

THE KING HATH HAPPILY RECEIVED, MACBETH, THE NEWS OF THY SUCCESS; AND WHEN HE READS THY PERSONAL VENTURE IN THE REBELS' FIGHT, HIS WONDERS AND HIS PRAISES DO CONTEND WHICH SHOULD BE THINE OR HIS. SILENCED WITH THAT, IN VIEWING O'ER THE REST O'THE SELFSAME DAY, HE FINDS THEE IN THE STOUT NORWEYAN RANKS, NOTHING AFEARD OF WHAT THYSELF DIDST MAKE, STRANGE IMAGES OF DEATH. AS THICK AS HAIL CAME POST WITH POST, AND EVERYONE DID BEAR THY PRAISES IN HIS KINGDOM'S GREAT DEFENCE, AND POURED THEM DOWN BEFORE HIM.

WE ARE SENT TO GIVE THEE FROM OUR ROYAL MASTER THANKS; ONLY TO HERALD THEE INTO HIS SIGHT, NOT PAY THEE.

AND, FOR AN EARNEST OF A GREATER HONOUR, HE BADE ME, FROM HIM, CALL THEE THANE OF CAWDOR: IN WHICH ADDITION, HAIL, MOST WORTHY THANE, FOR IT IS THINE.

THE THANE OF CAWDOR LIVES: WHY DO YOU DRESS ME IN BORROWED ROBES?

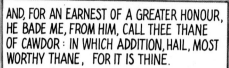

WHAT! CAN THE DEVIL SPEAK TRUE?

WHO WAS THE THANE LIVES YET; BUT UNDER HEAVY JUDGEMENT BEARS THAT LIFE WHICH HE DESERVES TO LOSE. WHETHER HE WAS COMBINED WITH THOSE OF NORWAY, OR DID LINE THE REBEL WITH HIDDEN HELP AND VANTAGE, OR THAT WITH BOTH HE LABOURED IN HIS COUNTRY'S WRACK, I KNOW NOT; BUT TREASONS CAPITAL, CONFESSED AND PROVED, HAVE OVERTHROWN HIM.

GLAMIS, AND THANE OF CAWDOR! THE GREATEST IS BEHIND.

THANKS FOR YOUR PAINS. — DO YOU NOT HOPE YOUR CHILDREN SHALL BE KINGS, WHEN THOSE THAT GAVE THE THANE OF CAWDOR TO ME PROMISED NO LESS TO THEM?

THAT, TRUSTED HOME, MIGHT YET ENKINDLE YOU UNTO THE CROWN, BESIDES THE THANE OF CAWDOR. BUT 'TIS STRANGE: AND OFTENTIMES, TO WIN US TO OUR HARM, THE INSTRUMENTS OF DARKNESS TELL US TRUTHS, WIN US WITH HONEST TRIFLES, TO BETRAY'S IN DEEPEST CONSEQUENCE. COUSINS, A WORD, I PRAY YOU.

TWO TRUTHS ARE TOLD, AS HAPPY PROLOGUES TO THE SWELLING ACT OF THE IMPERIAL THEME.

I THANK YOU, GENTLEMEN.

THIS SUPERNATURAL SOLICITING CANNOT BE ILL, CANNOT BE GOOD. IF ILL, WHY HATH IT GIVEN ME EARNEST OF SUCCESS, COMMENCING IN A TRUTH? I AM THANE OF CAWDOR. IF GOOD, WHY DO I YIELD TO THAT SUGGESTION WHOSE HORRID IMAGE DOTH...

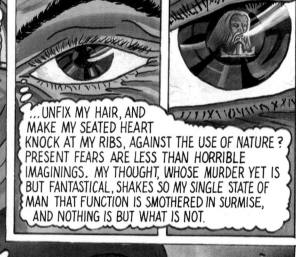

...UNFIX MY HAIR, AND MAKE MY SEATED HEART KNOCK AT MY RIBS, AGAINST THE USE OF NATURE? PRESENT FEARS ARE LESS THAN HORRIBLE IMAGININGS. MY THOUGHT, WHOSE MURDER YET IS BUT FANTASTICAL, SHAKES SO MY SINGLE STATE OF MAN THAT FUNCTION IS SMOTHERED IN SURMISE, AND NOTHING IS BUT WHAT IS NOT.

LOOK, HOW OUR PARTNER'S RAPT.

IF CHANCE WILL HAVE ME KING, WHY, CHANCE MAY CROWN ME, WITHOUT MY STIR.

NEW HONOURS COME UPON HIM, LIKE OUR STRANGE GARMENTS, CLEAVE NOT TO THEIR MOULD BUT WITH THE AID OF USE.

COME WHAT COME MAY, TIME AND THE HOUR RUNS THROUGH THE ROUGHEST DAY.

WORTHY MACBETH, WE STAY UPON YOUR LEISURE.

GIVE ME YOUR FAVOUR: MY DULL BRAIN WAS WROUGHT WITH THINGS FORGOTTEN. KIND GENTLEMEN, YOUR PAINS ARE REGISTERED WHERE EVERY DAY I TURN THE LEAF TO READ THEM. LET US TOWARD THE KING.

VERY GLADLY.

THINK UPON WHAT HATH CHANCED; AND AT MORE TIME, THE INTERIM HAVING WEIGHED IT, LET US SPEAK OUR FREE HEARTS EACH TO OTHER.

TILL THEN, ENOUGH. COME, FRIENDS.

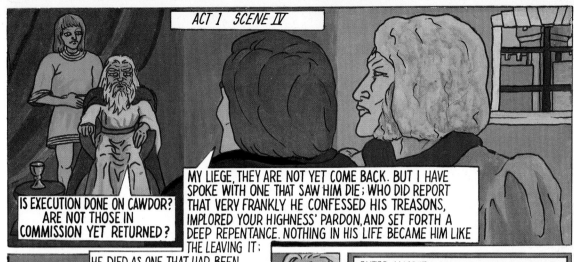

IS EXECUTION DONE ON CAWDOR? ARE NOT THOSE IN COMMISSION YET RETURNED?

MY LIEGE, THEY ARE NOT YET COME BACK. BUT I HAVE SPOKE WITH ONE THAT SAW HIM DIE; WHO DID REPORT THAT VERY FRANKLY HE CONFESSED HIS TREASONS, IMPLORED YOUR HIGHNESS' PARDON, AND SET FORTH A DEEP REPENTANCE. NOTHING IN HIS LIFE BECAME HIM LIKE THE LEAVING IT;

HE DIED AS ONE THAT HAD BEEN STUDIED IN HIS DEATH TO THROW AWAY THE DEAREST THING HE OWED, AS 'TWERE A CARELESS TRIFLE.

THERE'S NO ART TO FIND THE MIND'S CONSTRUCTION IN THE FACE: HE WAS A GENTLEMAN ON WHOM I BUILT AN ABSOLUTE TRUST.

ENTER MACBETH, BANQUO, ROSS AND ANGUS

O WORTHIEST COUSIN!

THE SIN OF MY INGRATITUDE EVEN NOW WAS HEAVY ON ME. THOU ART SO FAR BEFORE, THAT SWIFTEST WING OF RECOMPENSE IS SLOW TO OVERTAKE THEE. WOULD THOU HADST LESS DESERVED, THAT THE PROPORTION BOTH OF THANKS AND PAYMENT MIGHT HAVE BEEN MINE! ONLY I HAVE LEFT TO SAY, MORE IS THY DUE THAN MORE THAN ALL CAN PAY.

THE SERVICE AND THE LOYALTY I OWE, IN DOING IT, PAYS ITSELF. YOUR HIGHNESS' PART IS TO RECEIVE OUR DUTIES: AND OUR DUTIES ARE TO YOUR THRONE AND STATE, CHILDREN AND SERVANTS; WHICH DO BUT WHAT THEY SHOULD, BY DOING EVERYTHING SAFE TOWARD YOUR LOVE AND HONOUR.

WELCOME HITHER: I HAVE BEGUN TO PLANT THEE, AND WILL LABOUR TO MAKE THEE FULL OF GROWING. NOBLE BANQUO, THAT HAST NO LESS DESERVED, NOR MUST BE KNOWN NO LESS TO HAVE DONE SO, LET ME ENFOLD THEE AND HOLD THEE TO MY HEART.

THERE IF I GROW, THE HARVEST IS YOUR OWN.

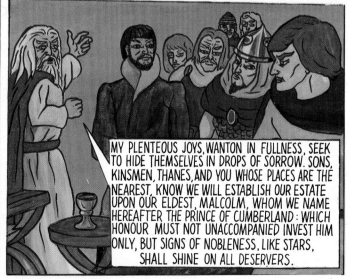

MY PLENTEOUS JOYS, WANTON IN FULLNESS, SEEK TO HIDE THEMSELVES IN DROPS OF SORROW. SONS, KINSMEN, THANES, AND YOU WHOSE PLACES ARE THE NEAREST, KNOW WE WILL ESTABLISH OUR ESTATE UPON OUR ELDEST, MALCOLM, WHOM WE NAME HEREAFTER THE PRINCE OF CUMBERLAND: WHICH HONOUR MUST NOT UNACCOMPANIED INVEST HIM ONLY, BUT SIGNS OF NOBLENESS, LIKE STARS, SHALL SHINE ON ALL DESERVERS.

FROM HENCE TO INVERNESS, AND BIND US FURTHER TO YOU.

THE REST IS LABOUR, WHICH IS NOT USED FOR YOU. I'LL BE MYSELF THE HARBINGER AND MAKE JOYFUL THE HEARING OF MY WIFE WITH YOUR APPROACH; SO HUMBLY TAKE MY LEAVE.

MY WORTHY CAWDOR!

THE PRINCE OF CUMBERLAND! THAT IS A STEP ON WHICH I MUST FALL DOWN, OR ELSE O'ER-LEAP, FOR IN MY WAY IT LIES. STARS, HIDE YOUR FIRES! LET NOT LIGHT SEE MY BLACK AND DEEP DESIRES: THE EYE WINK AT THE HAND; YET LET THAT BE WHICH THE EYE FEARS, WHEN IT IS DONE, TO SEE.

TRUE, WORTHY BANQUO; HE IS FULL SO VALIANT, AND IN HIS COMMENDATIONS I AM FED; IT IS A BANQUET TO ME.

EXIT MACBETH

LET'S AFTER HIM, WHOSE CARE IS GONE BEFORE TO BID US WELCOME. IT IS A PEERLESS KINSMAN.

They met me in the day of success; and I have learned by the perfectest report, they have more in them than mortal knowledge.

When I burned in desire to question them further, they made themselves air, into which they vanished. Whiles I stood rapt in the wonder of it, came missives from the king, who all-hailed me, 'Thane of Cawdor'; by which title before, these weird sisters saluted me, and referred me to the coming on of time, with 'Hail King that shalt be!' This have I thought good to deliver thee, my dearest partner of greatness, that thou mightest not lose the dues of rejoicing by being ignorant of what greatness is promised thee.
Lay it to thy heart, and farewell.

Macbeth

GLAMIS THOU ART, AND CAWDOR, AND SHALT BE WHAT THOU ART PROMISED. YET DO I FEAR THY NATURE: IT IS TOO FULL O'THE MILK OF HUMAN KINDNESS TO CATCH THE NEAREST WAY. THOU WOULDST BE GREAT, ART NOT WITHOUT AMBITION, BUT WITHOUT THE ILLNESS SHOULD ATTEND IT. WHAT THOU WOULDST HIGHLY, THAT WOULDST THOU HOLILY; WOULDST NOT PLAY FALSE, AND YET WOULDST WRONGLY WIN. THOU'DST HAVE, GREAT GLAMIS, THAT WHICH CRIES, 'THUS THOU MUST DO' IF THOU HAVE IT, AND THAT WHICH RATHER THOU DOST FEAR TO DO THAN WISHEST SHOULD BE UNDONE. HIE THEE HITHER,

COME, YOU SPIRITS
THAT TEND ON MORTAL THOUGHTS! UNSEX ME HERE,
AND FILL ME, FROM THE CROWN TO THE TOE, TOP-FULL
OF DIREST CRUELTY! MAKE THICK MY BLOOD,
STOP UP THE ACCESS AND PASSAGE TO REMORSE,
THAT NO COMPUNCTIOUS VISITINGS OF NATURE
SHAKE MY FELL PURPOSE, NOR KEEP PEACE BETWEEN
THE EFFECT AND IT! COME TO MY WOMAN'S BREASTS,
AND TAKE MY MILK FOR GALL, YOU MURDERING MINISTERS,
WHEREVER IN YOUR SIGHTLESS SUBSTANCES
YOU WAIT ON NATURE'S MISCHIEF! COME, THICK NIGHT,
AND PALL THEE IN THE DUNNEST SMOKE OF HELL,
THAT MY KEEN KNIFE SEE NOT THE WOUND IT MAKES,
NOR HEAVEN PEEP THROUGH THE BLANKET OF THE DARK,
TO CRY, 'HOLD, HOLD!'

.ENTER MACBETH

GREAT GLAMIS! WORTHY CAWDOR! GREATER THAN BOTH BY THE ALL-HAIL HEREAFTER! THY LETTERS HAVE TRANSPORTED ME BEYOND THIS IGNORANT PRESENT, AND I FEEL NOW THE FUTURE IN THE INSTANT.

MY DEAREST LOVE, DUNCAN COMES HERE TONIGHT.

AND WHEN GOES HENCE?

TOMORROW, AS HE PURPOSES.

O NEVER SHALL SUN THAT MORROW SEE!

YOUR FACE, MY THANE, IS AS A BOOK WHERE MEN MAY READ STRANGE MATTERS.

TO BEGUILE THE TIME, LOOK LIKE THE TIME; BEAR WELCOME IN YOUR EYE, YOUR HAND, YOUR TONGUE: LOOK LIKE THE INNOCENT FLOWER, BUT BE THE SERPENT UNDER'T. HE THAT'S COMING MUST BE PROVIDED FOR; AND YOU SHALL PUT THIS NIGHT'S GREAT BUSINESS INTO MY DISPATCH, WHICH SHALL TO ALL OUR NIGHTS AND DAYS TO COME GIVE SOLELY SOVEREIGN SWAY AND MASTERDOM.

WE WILL SPEAK FURTHER.

ONLY LOOK UP CLEAR: TO ALTER FAVOUR EVER IS TO FEAR. LEAVE ALL THE REST TO ME.

SEE, SEE, OUR HONOURED HOSTESS! THE LOVE THAT FOLLOWS US SOMETIME IS OUR TROUBLE, WHICH STILL WE THANK AS LOVE. HEREIN I TEACH YOU HOW YOU SHALL BID GOD 'IELD US FOR YOUR PAINS, AND THANK US FOR YOUR TROUBLE.

ALL OUR SERVICE IN EVERY POINT TWICE DONE, AND THEN DONE DOUBLE, WERE POOR AND SINGLE BUSINESS TO CONTEND AGAINST THOSE HONOURS DEEP AND BROAD

WHEREWITH YOUR MAJESTY LOADS OUR HOUSE: FOR THOSE OF OLD, AND THE LATE DIGNITIES HEAPED UP TO THEM, WE REST YOUR HERMITS.

WHERE'S THE THANE OF CAWDOR? WE COURSED HIM AT THE HEELS, AND HAD A PURPOSE TO BE HIS PURVEYOR: BUT HE RIDES WELL, AND HIS GREAT LOVE, SHARP AS HIS SPUR, HATH HOLP HIM TO HIS HOME BEFORE US. FAIR AND NOBLE HOSTESS, WE ARE YOUR GUEST TONIGHT.

GIVE ME YOUR HAND: CONDUCT ME TO MINE HOST. WE LOVE HIM HIGHLY, AND SHALL CONTINUE OUR GRACES TOWARDS HIM.

BY YOUR LEAVE, HOSTESS.

YOUR SERVANTS EVER HAVE THEIRS, THEMSELVES, AND WHAT IS THEIRS, IN COMPT, TO MAKE THEIR AUDIT AT YOUR HIGHNESS' PLEASURE, STILL TO RETURN YOUR OWN.

IF IT WERE DONE WHEN 'TIS DONE, THEN 'TWERE WELL IT WERE DONE QUICKLY. IF THE ASSASSINATION COULD TRAMMEL UP THE CONSEQUENCE, AND CATCH WITH HIS SURCEASE SUCCESS; THAT BUT THIS BLOW MIGHT BE THE BE-ALL AND THE END-ALL. HERE, BUT HERE, UPON THIS BANK AND SHOAL OF TIME, WE'D JUMP THE LIFE TO COME.

BUT IN THESE CASES WE STILL HAVE JUDGEMENT HERE; THAT WE BUT TEACH BLOODY INSTRUCTIONS, WHICH, BEING TAUGHT, RETURN TO PLAGUE THE INVENTOR. THIS EVEN-HANDED JUSTICE COMMENDS THE INGREDIENCE OF OUR POISONED CHALICE TO OUR OWN LIPS. HE'S HERE IN DOUBLE TRUST: FIRST, AS I AM HIS KINSMAN AND HIS SUBJECT, STRONG BOTH AGAINST THE DEED; THEN, AS HIS HOST,

TRUMPET-TONGUED AGAINST THE DEEP DAMNATION OF HIS TAKING-OFF; AND PITY, LIKE A NAKED NEW-BORN BABE, STRIDING THE BLAST, OR HEAVEN'S CHERUBIN, HORSED UPON THE SIGHTLESS COURIERS OF THE AIR, SHALL BLOW THE HORRID DEED IN EVERY EYE, THAT TEARS SHALL DROWN THE WIND.

WHO SHOULD AGAINST HIS MURDERER SHUT THE DOOR, NOT BEAR THE KNIFE MYSELF. BESIDES, THIS DUNCAN HATH BORNE HIS FACULTIES SO MEEK, HATH BEEN SO CLEAR IN HIS GREAT OFFICE, THAT HIS VIRTUES WILL PLEAD LIKE ANGELS

I HAVE NO SPUR TO PRICK THE SIDES OF MY INTENT, BUT ONLY VAULTING AMBITION WHICH O'ER-LEAPS ITSELF AND FALLS ON THE OTHER.

ENTER LADY MACBETH

HOW NOW! WHAT NEWS?

HE HAS ALMOST SUPPED: WHY HAVE YOU LEFT THE CHAMBER?

HATH HE ASKED FOR ME?

KNOW YOU NOT HE HAS?

WE WILL PROCEED NO FURTHUR IN THIS BUSINESS: HE HATH HONOURED ME OF LATE, AND I HAVE BOUGHT GOLDEN OPINIONS FROM ALL SORTS OF PEOPLE, WHICH WOULD BE WORN NOW IN THEIR NEWEST GLOSS, NOT CAST ASIDE SO SOON.

WAS THE HOPE DRUNK WHEREIN YOU DRESSED YOURSELF? HATH IT SLEPT SINCE? AND WAKES IT NOW, TO LOOK SO GREEN AND PALE AT WHAT IT DID SO FREELY? FROM THIS TIME SUCH I ACCOUNT THY LOVE. ART THOU AFEARED TO BE THE SAME IN THINE OWN ACT AND VALOUR AS THOU ART IN DESIRE? WOULDST THOU HAVE THAT WHICH THOU ESTEEM'ST THE ORNAMENT OF LIFE, AND LIVE A COWARD IN THINE OWN ESTEEM, LETTING 'I DARE NOT' WAIT UPON 'I WOULD', LIKE THE POOR CAT I' THE ADAGE?

WHAT BEAST WAS'T THEN THAT MADE YOU BREAK THIS ENTERPRISE TO ME? WHEN YOU DURST DO IT, THEN YOU WERE A MAN; AND, TO BE MORE THAN WHAT YOU WERE, YOU WOULD BE SO MUCH MORE THE MAN. NOR TIME NOR PLACE DID THEN ADHERE, AND YET YOU WOULD MAKE BOTH: THEY HAVE MADE THEMSELVES, AND THAT THEIR FITNESS NOW DOES UNMAKE YOU. I HAVE GIVEN SUCK, AND KNOW HOW TENDER 'TIS TO LOVE THE BABE THAT MILKS ME: I WOULD, WHILE IT WAS SMILING IN MY FACE, HAVE PLUCKED MY NIPPLE FROM HIS BONELESS GUMS AND DASHED THE BRAINS OUT, HAD I SO SWORN AS YOU HAVE DONE TO THIS.

PRITHEE, PEACE. I DARE DO ALL THAT MAY BECOME A MAN; WHO DARES DO MORE IS NONE.

IF WE SHOULD FAIL?

WE FAIL!

BUT SCREW YOUR COURAGE TO THE STICKING PLACE, AND WE'LL NOT FAIL. WHEN DUNCAN IS ASLEEP- WHERETO THE RATHER SHALL HIS DAY'S HARD JOURNEY SOUNDLY INVITE HIM-HIS TWO CHAMBERLAINS WILL I WITH WINE AND WASSAIL SO CONVINCE, THAT MEMORY, THE WARDER OF THE BRAIN, SHALL BE A-FUME, AND THE RECEIPT OF

REASON A LIMBECK ONLY. WHEN IN SWINISH SLEEP THEIR DRENCHED NATURES LIES AS IN A DEATH, WHAT CANNOT YOU AND I PERFORM UPON THE UNGUARDED DUNCAN ? WHAT NOT PUT UPON HIS SPONGY OFFICERS, WHO SHALL BEAR THE GUILT OF OUR GREAT QUELL ?

BRING FORTH MEN-CHILDREN ONLY : FOR THY UNDAUNTED METTLE SHOULD COMPOSE NOTHING BUT MALES.

WILL IT NOT BE RECEIVED, WHEN WE HAVE MARKED WITH BLOOD THOSE SLEEPY TWO OF HIS OWN CHAMBER, AND USED THEIR VERY DAGGERS, THAT THEY HAVE DONE'T ?

I AM SETTLED; AND BEND UP EACH CORPORAL AGENT TO THIS TERRIBLE FEAT. AWAY, AND MOCK THE TIME WITH FAIREST SHOW: FALSE FACE MUST HIDE WHAT THE FALSE HEART DOTH KNOW.

WHO DARES RECEIVE IT OTHER, AS WE SHALL MAKE OUR GRIEFS AND CLAMOUR ROAR UPON HIS DEATH ?

ACT II SCENE 1

HOW GOES THE NIGHT, BOY?

THE MOON IS DOWN; I HAVE NOT HEARD THE CLOCK.

AND SHE GOES DOWN AT TWELVE.

I TAKE'T, 'TIS LATER, SIR.

ENTER BANQUO AND FLEANCE

HOLD, TAKE MY SWORD. THERE'S HUSBANDRY IN HEAVEN: THEIR CANDLES ARE ALL OUT. TAKE THEE THAT TOO. A HEAVY SUMMONS LIES LIKE LEAD UPON ME, AND YET I WOULD NOT SLEEP. MERCIFUL POWERS, RESTRAIN IN ME THE CURSÈD THOUGHTS THAT NATURE GIVES WAY TO IN REPOSE!

GIVE ME MY SWORD.— WHO'S THERE?

ENTER MACBETH AND A SERVANT

A FRIEND.

WHAT, SIR, NOT YET AT REST? THE KING'S A-BED. HE HATH BEEN IN UNUSUAL PLEASURE, AND SENT FORTH GREAT LARGESS TO YOUR OFFICES. THIS DIAMOND HE GREETS YOUR WIFE WITHAL, BY THE NAME OF MOST KIND HOSTESS; AND SHUT UP IN MEASURELESS CONTENT.

BEING UNPREPARED, OUR WILL BECAME THE SERVANT TO DEFECT, WHICH ELSE SHOULD FREE HAVE WROUGHT.

ALL'S WELL. I DREAMT LAST NIGHT OF THE THREE WEIRD SISTERS: TO YOU THEY HAVE SHOWED SOME TRUTH.

I THINK NOT OF THEM: YET, WHEN WE CAN ENTREAT AN HOUR TO SERVE, WE WOULD SPEND IT IN SOME WORDS UPON THAT BUSINESS, IF YOU WOULD GRANT THE TIME.

AT YOUR KIND'ST LEISURE.

IF YOU SHALL CLEAVE TO MY CONSENT WHEN 'TIS, IT SHALL MAKE HONOUR FOR YOU.

SO I LOSE NONE IN SEEKING TO AUGMENT IT, BUT STILL KEEP MY BOSOM FRANCHISED AND ALLEGIANCE CLEAR, I SHALL BE COUNSELLED.

GOOD REPOSE THE WHILE!

THANKS, SIR; THE LIKE TO YOU.

GO BID THY MISTRESS, WHEN MY DRINK IS READY SHE STRIKE UPON THE BELL. GET THEE TO BED.

IT IS THE BLOODY BUSINESS WHICH INFORMS THUS TO MINE EYES. NOW O'ER THE ONE HALF-WORLD NATURE SEEMS DEAD, AND WICKED DREAMS ABUSE THE CURTAINED SLEEP. WITCHCRAFT CELEBRATES PALE HECATE'S OFFERINGS; AND WITHERED MURDER,

ALARUMED BY HIS SENTINEL, THE WOLF, WHOSE HOWL'S HIS WATCH, THUS WITH HIS STEALTHY PACE, WITH TARQUIN'S RAVISHING STRIDES, TOWARDS HIS DESIGN MOVES LIKE A GHOST.

THOU SURE AND FIRM-SET EARTH, HEAR NOT MY STEPS, WHICH WAY THEY WALK, FOR FEAR THY VERY STONES PRATE OF MY WHEREABOUT, AND TAKE THE PRESENT HORROR FROM THE TIME WHICH NOW SUITS WITH IT. — WHILES I THREAT HE LIVES:

WORDS TO THE HEAT OF DEEDS TOO COLD BREATH GIVES.

— A BELL RINGS.

I GO, AND IT IS DONE; THE BELL INVITES ME.

HEAR IT NOT, DUNCAN, FOR IT IS A KNELL THAT SUMMONS THEE TO HEAVEN, OR TO HELL.

ACT II SCENE II

THAT WHICH HATH MADE THEM DRUNK HATH MADE ME BOLD; WHAT HATH QUENCHED THEM HATH GIVEN ME FIRE. HARK! PEACE!

IT WAS THE OWL THAT SHRIEKED, THE FATAL BELLMAN, WHICH GIVES THE STERN'ST GOODNIGHT. HE IS ABOUT IT. THE DOORS ARE OPEN, AND THE SURFEITED GROOMS DO MOCK THEIR CHARGE WITH SNORES: I HAVE DRUGGED THEIR POSSETS, THAT DEATH AND NATURE DO CONTEND ABOUT THEM, WHETHER THEY LIVE OR DIE.

WHO'S THERE? WHAT, HO!

ALACK! I AM AFRAID THEY HAVE AWAKED AND 'TIS NOT DONE: THE ATTEMPT AND NOT THE DEED CONFOUNDS US. HARK! I LAID THEIR DAGGERS READY; HE COULD NOT MISS 'EM. HAD HE NOT RESEMBLED MY FATHER AS HE SLEPT, I HAD DONE'T.

MY HUSBAND!

I HAVE DONE THE DEED. DIDST THOU NOT HEAR A NOISE?

I HEARD THE OWL SCREAM AND THE CRICKETS CRY. DID YOU NOT SPEAK?

WHEN?

NOW.

AS I DESCENDED?

AY.

HARK! WHO LIES I' THE SECOND CHAMBER? DONALBAIN.

THIS IS A SORRY SIGHT.

A FOOLISH THOUGHT, TO SAY A SORRY SIGHT.

THERE'S ONE DID LAUGH IN'S SLEEP, AND ONE CRIED 'MURDER!' THAT THEY DID WAKE EACH OTHER. I STOOD AND HEARD THEM. BUT THEY DID SAY THEIR PRAYERS, AND ADDRESSED THEM AGAIN TO SLEEP.

THERE ARE TWO LODGED TOGETHER.

ONE CRIED 'GOD BLESS US!' AND 'AMEN' THE OTHER, AS THEY HAD SEEN ME WITH THESE HANGMAN'S HANDS. LISTENING THEIR FEAR, I COULD NOT SAY 'AMEN', WHEN THEY DID SAY 'GOD BLESS US!'

CONSIDER IT NOT SO DEEPLY.

BUT WHEREFORE COULD I NOT PRONOUNCE 'AMEN'? I HAD MOST NEED OF BLESSING, AND 'AMEN' STUCK IN MY THROAT.

THESE DEEDS MUST NOT BE THOUGHT AFTER THESE WAYS; SO, IT WILL MAKE US MAD.

METHOUGHT I HEARD A VOICE CRY 'SLEEP NO MORE! MACBETH DOES MURDER SLEEP,'— THE INNOCENT SLEEP, SLEEP THAT KNITS UP THE RAVELLED SLEAVE OF CARE, THE DEATH OF EACH DAY'S LIFE, SORE LABOUR'S BATH, BALM OF HURT MINDS, GREAT NATURE'S SECOND COURSE, CHIEF NOURISHER IN LIFE'S FEAST,—

WHAT DO YOU MEAN?

STILL IT CRIED, 'SLEEP NO MORE!' TO ALL THE HOUSE: 'GLAMIS HATH MURDERED SLEEP, AND THEREFORE CAWDOR SHALL SLEEP NO MORE: MACBETH SHALL SLEEP NO MORE!'

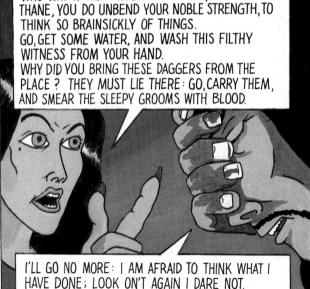

WHO WAS IT THAT THUS CRIED? WHY, WORTHY THANE, YOU DO UNBEND YOUR NOBLE STRENGTH, TO THINK SO BRAINSICKLY OF THINGS. GO, GET SOME WATER, AND WASH THIS FILTHY WITNESS FROM YOUR HAND. WHY DID YOU BRING THESE DAGGERS FROM THE PLACE? THEY MUST LIE THERE: GO, CARRY THEM, AND SMEAR THE SLEEPY GROOMS WITH BLOOD.

I'LL GO NO MORE: I AM AFRAID TO THINK WHAT I HAVE DONE; LOOK ON'T AGAIN I DARE NOT.

ACT II SCENE III

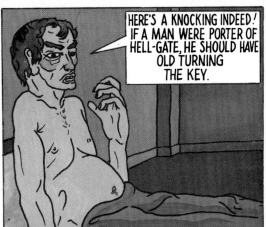

HERE'S A KNOCKING INDEED!
IF A MAN WERE PORTER OF
HELL-GATE, HE SHOULD HAVE
OLD TURNING
THE KEY.

KNOCK, KNOCK, KNOCK!
WHO'S THERE, I'THE NAME OF
BEELZEBUB? HERE'S A FARMER THAT
HANGED HIMSELF ON THE EXPECTATION OF
PLENTY. COME IN TIME! HAVE NAPKINS ENOW
ABOUT YOU; HERE YOU'LL SWEAT FOR'T.

KNOCK, KNOCK! WHO'S THERE I'THE OTHER
DEVIL'S NAME? FAITH, HERE'S AN EQUIVOCATOR,
THAT COULD SWEAR IN BOTH THE SCALES
AGAINST EITHER SCALE;
WHO COMMITTED
TREASON ENOUGH FOR
GOD'S SAKE, YET COULD NOT
EQUIVOCATE TO HEAVEN. O!
COME IN, EQUIVOCATOR.

KNOCK, KNOCK, KNOCK!
WHO'S THERE? FAITH,
HERE'S AN ENGLISH TAILOR
COME HITHER FOR STEALING
OUT OF A FRENCH HOSE.
COME IN, TAILOR; HERE YOU
MAY ROAST YOUR GOOSE.

KNOCK, KNOCK; NEVER AT QUIET!
WHAT ARE YOU?—BUT THIS PLACE
IS TOO COLD FOR HELL.
I'LL DEVIL-PORTER IT NO FURTHER.

I HAD THOUGHT TO HAVE LET IN SOME OF
ALL PROFESSIONS THAT GO THE PRIMROSE WAY
TO THE EVERLASTING BONFIRE.

ANON, ANON! I PRAY YOU,
REMEMBER THE PORTER.

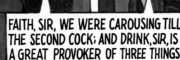

WAS IT SO LATE, FRIEND, ERE YOU WENT TO BED, THAT YOU DO LIE SO LATE?

FAITH, SIR, WE WERE CAROUSING TILL THE SECOND COCK; AND DRINK, SIR, IS A GREAT PROVOKER OF THREE THINGS.

WHAT THREE THINGS DOES DRINK ESPECIALLY PROVOKE?

MARRY, SIR, NOSE-PAINTING, SLEEP, AND URINE. LECHERY, SIR, IT PROVOKES, AND UNPROVOKES: IT PROVOKES THE DESIRE, BUT IT TAKES AWAY THE PERFORMANCE. THEREFORE MUCH DRINK MAY BE SAID TO BE AN EQUIVOCATOR WITH LECHERY: IT MAKES HIM, AND IT MARS HIM; IT SETS HIM ON, AND IT TAKES HIM OFF; IT PERSUADES HIM, AND DISHEARTENS HIM; MAKES HIM STAND TO, AND NOT STAND TO; IN CONCLUSION, EQUIVOCATES HIM IN A SLEEP, AND GIVING HIM THE LIE, LEAVES HIM.

I BELIEVE DRINK GAVE THEE THE LIE LAST NIGHT.

IS THY MASTER STIRRING? OUR KNOCKING HAS AWAKED HIM; HERE HE COMES.

THAT IT DID, SIR, I'THE VERY THROAT ON ME: BUT I REQUITED HIM FOR HIS LIE, AND, I THINK, BEING TOO STRONG FOR HIM, THOUGH HE TOOK UP MY LEGS SOMETIME, YET I MADE A SHIFT TO CAST HIM.

GOOD MORROW, NOBLE SIR.

GOOD MORROW, BOTH.

IS THE KING STIRRING, WORTHY THANE?

NOT YET.

HE DID COMMAND ME TO CALL TIMELY ON HIM: I HAVE ALMOST SLIPPED THE HOUR.

I'LL BRING YOU TO HIM.

I KNOW THIS IS A JOYFUL TROUBLE TO YOU; BUT YET 'TIS ONE.

THE LABOUR WE DELIGHT IN PHYSICS PAIN. THIS IS THE DOOR.

I'LL MAKE SO BOLD TO CALL, FOR 'TIS MY LIMITED SERVICE.

GOES THE KING HENCE TODAY?

HE DOES: HE DID APPOINT SO.

THE NIGHT HAS BEEN UNRULY: WHERE WE LAY, OUR CHIMNEYS WERE BLOWN DOWN, AND, AS THEY SAY, LAMENTINGS HEARD I'THE AIR, STRANGE SCREAMS OF DEATH AND

PROPHESYING WITH ACCENTS TERRIBLE, OF DIRE COMBUSTION AND CONFUSED EVENTS NEW HATCHED TO THE WOEFUL TIME. THE OBSCURE BIRD CLAMOURED THE LIVELONG NIGHT: SOME SAY THE EARTH WAS FEVEROUS AND DID SHAKE.

'TWAS A ROUGH NIGHT.

MY YOUNG REMEMBRANCE CANNOT PARALLEL A FELLOW TO IT.

O HORROR!

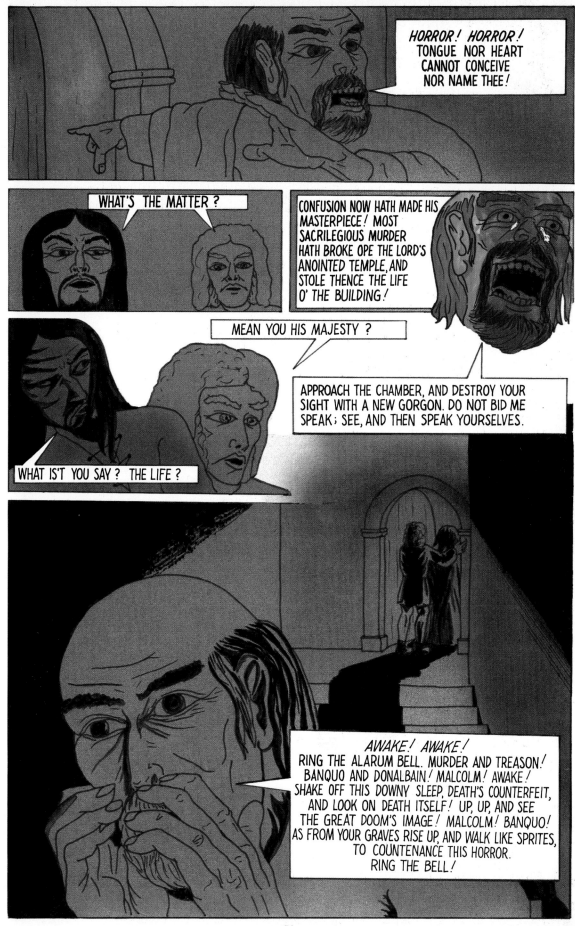

THOSE OF HIS CHAMBER, AS IT SEEMED, HAD DONE'T: THEIR HANDS AND FACES WERE ALL BADGED WITH BLOOD, SO WERE THEIR DAGGERS, WHICH, UNWIPED, WE FOUND UPON THEIR PILLOWS: THEY STARED, AND WERE DISTRACTED; NO MAN'S LIFE WAS TO BE TRUSTED WITH THEM.

O! YET I DO REPENT ME OF MY FURY, THAT I DID KILL THEM.

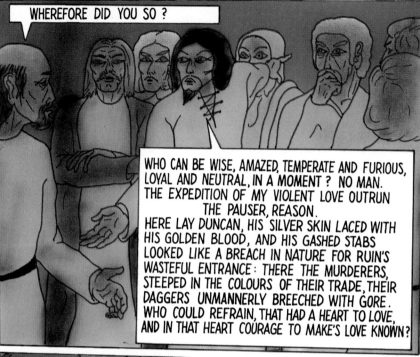

WHEREFORE DID YOU SO?

WHO CAN BE WISE, AMAZED, TEMPERATE AND FURIOUS, LOYAL AND NEUTRAL, IN A MOMENT? NO MAN. THE EXPEDITION OF MY VIOLENT LOVE OUTRUN THE PAUSER, REASON. HERE LAY DUNCAN, HIS SILVER SKIN LACED WITH HIS GOLDEN BLOOD, AND HIS GASHED STABS LOOKED LIKE A BREACH IN NATURE FOR RUIN'S WASTEFUL ENTRANCE: THERE THE MURDERERS, STEEPED IN THE COLOURS OF THEIR TRADE, THEIR DAGGERS UNMANNERLY BREECHED WITH GORE. WHO COULD REFRAIN, THAT HAD A HEART TO LOVE, AND IN THAT HEART COURAGE TO MAKE'S LOVE KNOWN?

HELP ME HENCE, HO!

LOOK TO THE LADY!

WHY DO WE HOLD OUR TONGUES, THAT MOST MAY CLAIM THIS ARGUMENT FOR OURS?

WHAT SHOULD BE SPOKEN HERE, WHERE OUR FATE, HID IN AN AUGER-HOLE, MAY RUSH AND SEIZE US? LET'S AWAY: OUR TEARS ARE NOT YET BREWED.

NOR OUR STRONG SORROW UPON THE FOOT OF MOTION.

LOOK TO THE LADY.

AND WHEN WE HAVE OUR NAKED FRAILTIES HID, THAT SUFFER IN EXPOSURE, LET US MEET AND QUESTION THIS MOST BLOODY PIECE OF WORK, TO KNOW IT FURTHER. FEARS AND SCRUPLES SHAKE US. IN THE GREAT HAND OF GOD I STAND, AND THENCE AGAINST THE UNDIVULGED PRETENCE I FIGHT OF TREASONOUS MALICE.

AND SO DO I.

SO ALL.

LET'S BRIEFLY PUT ON MANLY READINESS, AND MEET I'THE HALL TOGETHER.

WELL CONTENTED.

WHAT WILL YOU DO ?
LET'S NOT CONSORT WITH THEM.
TO SHOW AN UNFELT SORROW
IS AN OFFICE WHICH
THE FALSE MAN DOES EASY.
I'LL TO ENGLAND.

TO IRELAND, I;
OUR SEPARATED FORTUNE
SHALL KEEP US BOTH THE SAFER.
WHERE WE ARE
THERE'S DAGGERS
IN MEN'S SMILES :
THE NEAR IN BLOOD,
THE NEARER BLOODY.

THIS MURDEROUS SHAFT THAT'S SHOT HATH NOT YET LIGHTED, AND OUR SAFEST WAY IS TO AVOID THE AIM. THEREFORE TO HORSE, AND LET US NOT BE DAINTY OF LEAVE-TAKING,

BUT SHIFT AWAY.
THERE'S WARRANT IN THAT THEFT
WHICH STEALS ITSELF
WHEN THERE'S NO MERCY LEFT.

ACT II SCENE IV

ENTER ROSS AND AN OLD MAN.

THREESCORE AND TEN I CAN REMEMBER WELL; WITHIN THE VOLUME OF WHICH TIME I HAVE SEEN HOURS DREADFUL AND THINGS STRANGE, BUT THIS SORE NIGHT HATH TRIFLED FORMER KNOWINGS.

'TIS UNNATURAL, EVEN LIKE THE DEED THAT'S DONE. ON TUESDAY LAST A FALCON, TOWERING IN HER PRIDE OF PLACE, WAS BY A MOUSING OWL HAWKED AT AND KILLED.

HA, GOOD FATHER, THOU SEEST THE HEAVENS, AS TROUBLED WITH MAN'S ACT, THREATENS HIS BLOODY STAGE. BY THE CLOCK 'TIS DAY, AND YET DARK NIGHT STRANGLES THE TRAVELLING LAMP: IS'T NIGHT'S PREDOMINANCE OR THE DAY'S SHAME, THAT DARKNESS DOES THE FACE OF EARTH ENTOMB, WHEN LIVING LIGHT SHOULD KISS IT?

AND DUNCAN'S HORSES—A THING MOST STRANGE AND CERTAIN—BEAUTEOUS AND SWIFT, THE MINIONS OF THEIR RACE, TURNED WILD IN NATURE, BROKE THEIR STALLS, FLUNG OUT, CONTENDING 'GAINST OBEDIENCE, AS THEY WOULD MAKE WAR WITH MANKIND.

'TIS SAID THEY EAT EACH OTHER.

THEY DID SO, TO THE AMAZEMENT OF MINE EYES THAT LOOKED UPON'T. HERE COMES THE GOOD MACDUFF. HOW GOES THE WORLD, SIR, NOW?

WHY, SEE YOU NOT?

IS'T KNOWN WHO DID THIS MORE THAN BLOODY DEED?

THOSE THAT MACBETH HATH SLAIN.

ALAS, THE DAY!

WHAT GOOD COULD THEY PRETEND?

THEY WERE SUBORNED. MALCOLM AND DONALBAIN, THE KING'S TWO SONS, ARE STOLEN AWAY AND FLED, WHICH PUTS UPON THEM SUSPICION OF THE DEED.

'GAINST NATURE STILL! THRIFTLESS AMBITION THAT WILL RAVIN UP THINE OWN LIFE'S MEANS! THEN 'TIS MOST LIKE THE SOVEREIGNTY WILL FALL UPON MACBETH.

HE IS ALREADY NAMED, AND GONE TO SCONE TO BE INVESTED.

WHERE IS DUNCAN'S BODY?

CARRIED TO COLMEKILL, THE SACRED STOREHOUSE OF HIS PREDECESSORS AND GUARDIAN OF THEIR BONES.

WILL YOU TO SCONE?

NO, COUSIN, I'LL TO FIFE.

WELL, I WILL THITHER.

WELL, MAY YOU SEE THINGS WELL DONE THERE: ADIEU! LEST OUR OLD ROBES SIT EASIER THAN OUR NEW!

FAREWELL, FATHER.

GOD'S BENISON GO WITH YOU, AND WITH THOSE THAT WOULD MAKE GOOD OF BAD, AND FRIENDS OF FOES!

ACT III SCENE I

THOU HAST IT NOW: KING, CAWDOR, GLAMIS, ALL, AS THE WEIRD WOMEN PROMISED; AND, I FEAR, THOU PLAYEDST MOST FOULLY FOR'T; YET IT WAS SAID IT SHOULD NOT STAND IN THY POSTERITY, BUT THAT MYSELF SHOULD BE THE ROOT AND FATHER OF MANY KINGS. IF THERE COME TRUTH FROM THEM, AS UPON THEE, MACBETH, THEIR SPEECHES SHINE, WHY, BY THE VERITIES ON THEE MADE GOOD, MAY THEY NOT BE MY ORACLES AS WELL, AND SET ME UP IN HOPE? BUT, HUSH! NO MORE.

HERE'S OUR CHIEF GUEST.

IF HE HAD BEEN FORGOTTEN, IT HAD BEEN AS A GAP IN OUR GREAT FEAST, AND ALL-THING UNBECOMING.

TONIGHT WE HOLD A SOLEMN SUPPER, SIR, AND I'LL REQUEST YOUR PRESENCE.

LET YOUR HIGHNESS COMMAND UPON ME, TO THE WHICH MY DUTIES ARE WITH A MOST INDISSOLUBLE TIE FOREVER KNIT.

RIDE YOU THIS AFTERNOON?

AY, MY GOOD LORD.

WE SHOULD HAVE ELSE DESIRED YOUR GOOD ADVICE, WHICH STILL HATH BEEN BOTH GRAVE AND PROSPEROUS, IN THIS DAY'S COUNCIL; BUT WE'LL TAKE TOMORROW. IS'T FAR YOU RIDE?

AS FAR, MY LORD, AS WILL FILL UP THE TIME 'TWIXT THIS AND SUPPER. GO NOT MY HORSE THE BETTER, I MUST BECOME A BORROWER OF THE NIGHT FOR A DARK HOUR OR TWAIN.

FAIL NOT OUR FEAST.

MY LORD, I WILL NOT.

WE HEAR OUR BLOODY COUSINS ARE BESTOWED IN ENGLAND AND IN IRELAND, NOT CONFESSING THEIR CRUEL PARRICIDE, FILLING THEIR HEARERS WITH STRANGE INVENTION. BUT OF THAT TOMORROW, WHEN THEREWITHAL WE SHALL HAVE CAUSE OF STATE CRAVING US JOINTLY. HIE YOU TO HORSE; ADIEU, TILL YOU RETURN AT NIGHT. GOES FLEANCE WITH YOU?

AY, MY GOOD LORD; OUR TIME DOES CALL UPON'S.

I WISH YOUR HORSES SWIFT AND SURE OF FOOT; AND SO I DO COMMEND YOU TO THEIR BACKS. FAREWELL.

LET EVERY MAN BE MASTER OF HIS TIME TILL SEVEN AT NIGHT. TO MAKE SOCIETY THE SWEETER WELCOME, WE WILL KEEP OURSELF TILL SUPPER-TIME ALONE. WHILE THEN, GOD BE WITH YOU!

SIRRAH, A WORD WITH YOU: ATTEND THOSE MEN OUR PLEASURE?

THEY ARE, MY LORD, WITHOUT THE PALACE GATE.

BRING THEM BEFORE US.

TO BE THUS IS NOTHING; BUT TO BE SAFELY THUS.— OUR FEARS IN BANQUO STICK DEEP, AND IN HIS ROYALTY OF NATURE REIGNS THAT WHICH WOULD BE FEARED.'TIS MUCH HE DARES, AND, TO THAT DAUNTLESS TEMPER OF HIS MIND, HE HATH A WISDOM THAT DOTH GUIDE HIS VALOUR TO ACT IN SAFETY. THERE IS NONE BUT HE WHOSE BEING I DO FEAR; AND UNDER HIM MY GENIUS IS REBUKED, AS IT IS SAID MARK ANTONY'S WAS BY CAESAR. HE CHID THE SISTERS WHEN FIRST THEY PUT THE NAME OF KING UPON ME, AND BADE THEM SPEAK TO HIM; THEN, PROPHET-LIKE, THEY HAILED HIM FATHER TO A LINE OF KINGS. UPON MY HEAD THEY PLACED A FRUITLESS CROWN, AND PUT A BARREN SCEPTRE IN MY GRIP,

THENCE TO BE WRENCHED WITH AN UNLINEAL HAND, NO SON OF MINE SUCCEEDING. IF IT BE SO, FOR BANQUO'S ISSUE HAVE I 'FILED MY MIND: FOR THEM THE GRACIOUS DUNCAN HAVE I MURDERED; PUT RANCOURS IN THE VESSEL OF MY PEACE, ONLY FOR THEM; AND MINE ETERNAL JEWEL GIVEN TO THE COMMON ENEMY OF MAN, TO MAKE THEM KINGS, THE SEED OF BANQUO KINGS! RATHER THAN SO, COME FATE INTO THE LIST AND CHAMPION ME TO THE UTTERANCE! WHO'S THERE?

NOW GO TO THE DOOR, AND STAY THERE TILL WE CALL.

WAS IT NOT YESTERDAY WE SPOKE TOGETHER?

IT WAS, SO PLEASE YOUR HIGHNESS.

WELL THEN, NOW HAVE YOU CONSIDERED OF MY SPEECHES? KNOW THAT IT WAS HE IN THE TIMES PAST WHICH HELD YOU SO UNDER FORTUNE, WHICH YOU THOUGHT HAD BEEN OUR INNOCENT SELF. THIS I MADE GOOD TO YOU IN OUR LAST CONFERENCE; PASSED IN PROBATION WITH YOU HOW YOU WERE BORNE IN HAND, HOW CROSSED, THE INSTRUMENTS, WHO WROUGHT WITH THEM, AND ALL THINGS ELSE THAT MIGHT TO HALF A SOUL AND TO A NOTION CRAZED SAY, 'THUS DID BANQUO.'

YOU MADE IT KNOWN TO US.

I DID SO; AND WENT FURTHER, WHICH IS NOW OUR POINT OF SECOND MEETING. DO YOU FIND YOUR PATIENCE SO PREDOMINANT IN YOUR NATURE THAT YOU CAN LET THIS GO? ARE YOU SO GOSPELLED, TO PRAY FOR THIS GOOD MAN AND FOR HIS ISSUE, WHOSE HEAVY HAND HATH BOWED YOU TO THE GRAVE AND BEGGARED YOURS FOR EVER?

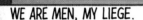

WE ARE MEN, MY LIEGE.

AY, IN THE CATALOGUE YE GO FOR MEN; AS HOUNDS AND GREYHOUNDS, MONGRELS, SPANIELS, CURS, SHOUGHS, WATER-RUGS, AND DEMI-WOLVES, ARE CLEPT ALL BY THE NAME OF DOGS. THE VALUED FILE DISTINGUISHES THE SWIFT, THE SLOW, THE SUBTLE, THE HOUSEKEEPER, THE HUNTER, EVERY ONE ACCORDING TO THE GIFT WHICH BOUNTEOUS NATURE HATH IN HIM CLOSED, WHEREBY HE DOES RECEIVE PARTICULAR ADDITION, FROM THE BILL THAT WRITES THEM ALL ALIKE: AND SO OF MEN. NOW, IF YOU HAVE A STATION IN THE FILE, NOT I'THE WORST RANK OF MANHOOD, SAY 'T; AND I WILL PUT THAT BUSINESS IN YOUR BOSOMS, WHOSE EXECUTION TAKES YOUR ENEMY OFF, GRAPPLES YOU TO THE HEART AND LOVE OF US, WHO WEAR OUR HEALTH BUT SICKLY IN HIS LIFE, WHICH IN HIS DEATH WERE PERFECT.

I AM ONE, MY LIEGE, WHOM THE VILE BLOWS AND BUFFETS OF THE WORLD HATH SO INCENSED THAT I AM RECKLESS WHAT I DO TO SPITE THE WORLD.

AND I ANOTHER, SO WEARY WITH DISASTERS, TUGGED WITH FORTUNE, THAT I WOULD SET MY LIFE ON ANY CHANCE, TO MEND IT OR BE RID ON'T.

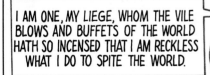

BOTH OF YOU KNOW BANQUO WAS YOUR ENEMY.

TRUE, MY LORD.

SO IS HE MINE, AND IN SUCH BLOODY DISTANCE THAT EVERY MINUTE OF HIS BEING THRUSTS AGAINST MY NEAREST OF LIFE: AND THOUGH I COULD WITH BARE-FACED POWER SWEEP HIM FROM MY SIGHT AND BID MY WILL AVOUCH IT, YET I MUST NOT, FOR CERTAIN FRIENDS THAT ARE BOTH HIS AND MINE, WHOSE LOVES I MAY NOT DROP, BUT WAIL HIS FALL WHO I MYSELF STRUCK DOWN: AND THENCE IT IS THAT I TO YOUR ASSISTANCE DO MAKE LOVE, MASKING THE BUSINESS FROM THE COMMON EYE FOR SUNDRY WEIGHTY REASONS.

WE SHALL, MY LORD, PERFORM WHAT YOU COMMAND US.

THOUGH OUR LIVES—

YOUR SPIRITS SHINE THROUGH YOU. WITHIN THIS HOUR AT MOST I WILL ADVISE YOU WHERE TO PLANT YOURSELVES, ACQUAINT YOU WITH THE PERFECT SPY O'THE TIME, THE MOMENT O'NT; FOR'T MUST BE DONE TONIGHT, AND SOMETHING FROM THE PALACE; ALWAYS THOUGHT THAT I REQUIRE A CLEARNESS: AND WITH HIM, TO LEAVE NO RUBS NOR BOTCHES IN THE WORK, FLEANCE HIS SON, THAT KEEPS HIM COMPANY, WHOSE ABSENCE IS NO LESS MATERIAL TO ME THAN IS HIS FATHER'S, MUST EMBRACE THE FATE OF THAT DARK HOUR. RESOLVE YOURSELVES APART; I'LL COME TO YOU ANON.

WE ARE RESOLVED, MY LORD.

I'LL CALL UPON YOU STRAIGHT: ABIDE WITHIN.

IT IS CONCLUDED: BANQUO, THY SOUL'S FLIGHT, IF IT FIND HEAVEN, MUST FIND IT OUT TONIGHT.

ACT III SCENE II

IS BANQUO GONE FROM COURT?

AY, MADAM, BUT RETURNS AGAIN TONIGHT.

SAY TO THE KING I WOULD ATTEND HIS LEISURE FOR A FEW WORDS.

MADAM, I WILL.

NOUGHT'S HAD, ALL'S SPENT, WHERE OUR DESIRE IS GOT WITHOUT CONTENT. 'TIS SAFER TO BE THAT WHICH WE DESTROY THAN BY DESTRUCTION DWELL IN DOUBTFUL JOY.

HOW NOW, MY LORD! WHY DO YOU KEEP ALONE, OF SORRIEST FANCIES YOUR COMPANIONS MAKING, USING THOSE THOUGHTS WHICH SHOULD INDEED HAVE DIED WITH THEM THEY THINK ON? THINGS WITHOUT ALL REMEDY SHOULD BE WITHOUT REGARD: WHAT'S DONE IS DONE.

WE HAVE SCORCHED THE SNAKE, NOT KILLED IT: SHE'LL CLOSE AND BE HERSELF, WHILST OUR POOR MALICE REMAINS IN DANGER OF HER FORMER TOOTH. BUT LET THE FRAME OF THINGS DISJOINT, BOTH THE WORLDS SUFFER, ERE WE WILL EAT OUR MEAL IN FEAR, AND SLEEP IN THE AFFLICTION OF THESE TERRIBLE DREAMS THAT SHAKE US NIGHTLY: BETTER BE WITH THE DEAD, WHOM WE, TO GAIN OUR PEACE, HAVE SENT TO PEACE, THAN ON THE TORTURE OF THE MIND TO LIE IN RESTLESS ECSTASY. DUNCAN IS IN HIS GRAVE; AFTER LIFE'S FITFUL FEVER HE SLEEPS WELL; TREASON HAS DONE HIS WORST: NOR STEEL, NOR POISON, MALICE DOMESTIC, FOREIGN LEVY, NOTHING CAN TOUCH HIM FURTHER.

COME ON; GENTLE MY LORD, SLEEK O'ER YOUR RUGGED LOOKS; BE BRIGHT AND JOVIAL AMONG YOUR GUESTS TONIGHT.

SO SHALL I, LOVE; AND SO, I PRAY, BE YOU. LET YOUR REMEMBRANCE APPLY TO BANQUO;

PRESENT HIM EMINENCE,
BOTH WITH EYE AND TONGUE:
UNSAFE THE WHILE, THAT WE MUST LAVE
OUR HONOURS IN THESE FLATTERING STREAMS,
AND MAKE OUR FACES VIZARDS TO OUR HEARTS,
DISGUISING WHAT THEY ARE.

YOU MUST LEAVE THIS.

O! FULL OF SCORPIONS IS MY MIND, DEAR WIFE;
THOU KNOW'ST THAT BANQUO AND HIS FLEANCE LIVES.

BUT IN THEM NATURE'S COPY'S NOT ETERNE.

THERE'S COMFORT YET; THEY ARE ASSAILABLE.
THEN BE THOU JOCUND. ERE THE BAT HATH FLOWN
HIS CLOISTERED FLIGHT, ERE TO BLACK HECATE'S
SUMMONS THE SHARD-BORNE BEETLE WITH HIS
DROWSY HUMS HATH RUNG NIGHT'S YAWNING PEAL,
THERE SHALL BE DONE A DEED OF DREADFUL NOTE.

WHAT'S TO BE DONE?

BE INNOCENT OF THE KNOWLEDGE, DEAREST CHUCK,
TILL THOU APPLAUD THE DEED. COME, SEELING NIGHT,
SCARF UP THE TENDER EYE OF PITIFUL DAY,
AND WITH THY BLOODY AND INVISIBLE HAND
CANCEL AND TEAR TO PIECES THAT GREAT BOND
WHICH KEEPS ME PALE!
LIGHT THICKENS, AND THE CROW MAKES WING TO
THE ROOKY WOOD: GOOD THINGS OF DAY BEGIN TO
DROOP AND DROWSE, WHILES NIGHT'S BLACK
AGENTS TO THEIR PREYS DO ROUSE.
THOU MARVELL'ST AT MY WORDS: BUT HOLD THEE STILL;
THINGS BAD BEGUN MAKE STRONG THEMSELVES BY ILL.
SO, PRITHEE, GO WITH ME.

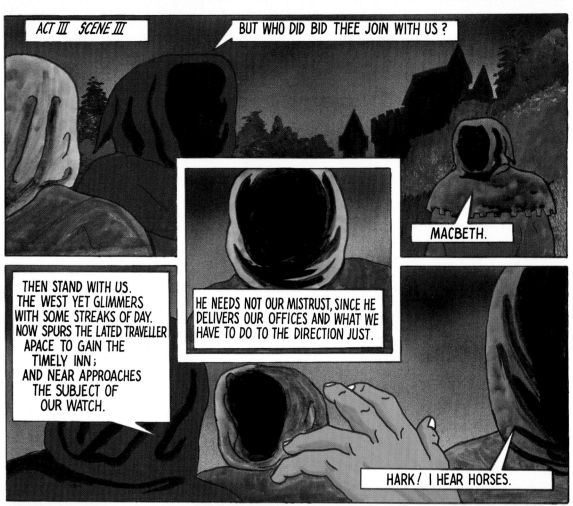

ACT III SCENE III

BUT WHO DID BID THEE JOIN WITH US?

MACBETH.

HE NEEDS NOT OUR MISTRUST, SINCE HE DELIVERS OUR OFFICES AND WHAT WE HAVE TO DO TO THE DIRECTION JUST.

THEN STAND WITH US. THE WEST YET GLIMMERS WITH SOME STREAKS OF DAY. NOW SPURS THE LATED TRAVELLER APACE TO GAIN THE TIMELY INN; AND NEAR APPROACHES THE SUBJECT OF OUR WATCH.

HARK! I HEAR HORSES.

GIVE US A LIGHT THERE, HO!

THEN 'TIS HE: THE REST THAT ARE WITHIN THE NOTE OF EXPECTATION ALREADY ARE I'THE COURT.

HIS HORSES GO ABOUT.

ALMOST A MILE: BUT HE DOES USUALLY, SO ALL MEN DO, FROM HENCE TO THE PALACE GATE MAKE IT THEIR WALK.

A LIGHT, A LIGHT!

'TIS HE.

STAND TO'T.

IT WILL BE RAIN TONIGHT.

LET IT COME DOWN.

O TREACHERY! FLY, GOOD FLEANCE, FLY, FLY, FLY! THOU MAYST REVENGE. O SLAVE!

44

YOU KNOW YOUR OWN DEGREES, SIT DOWN: AT FIRST AND LAST, THE HEARTY WELCOME.

THANKS TO YOUR MAJESTY.

OURSELF WILL MINGLE WITH SOCIETY AND PLAY THE HUMBLE HOST. OUR HOSTESS KEEPS HER STATE, BUT IN BEST TIME WE WILL REQUIRE HER WELCOME.

PRONOUNCE IT FOR ME, SIR, TO ALL OUR FRIENDS, FOR MY HEART SPEAKS THEY ARE WELCOME.

SEE, THEY ENCOUNTER THEE WITH THEIR HEARTS' THANKS; BOTH SIDES ARE EVEN. HERE, I'LL SIT I'THE MIDST. BE LARGE IN MIRTH; ANON WE'LL DRINK A MEASURE THE TABLE ROUND.

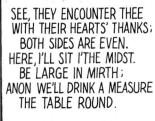

THERE'S BLOOD UPON THY FACE!

'TIS BANQUO'S THEN.

'TIS BETTER THEE WITHOUT THAN HE WITHIN. IS HE DISPATCHED?

MY LORD, HIS THROAT IS CUT; THAT I DID FOR HIM.

THOU ART THE BEST O' THE CUT-THROATS. YET HE'S GOOD THAT DID THE LIKE FOR FLEANCE. IF THOU DIDST IT, THOU ART THE NONPAREIL.

AY, MY GOOD LORD; SAFE IN A DITCH HE BIDES, WITH TWENTY TRENCHÈD GASHES ON HIS HEAD, THE LEAST A DEATH TO NATURE.

MOST ROYAL SIR- FLEANCE IS 'SCAPED.

THEN COMES MY FIT AGAIN: I HAD ELSE BEEN PERFECT; WHOLE AS THE MARBLE, FOUNDED AS THE ROCK, AS BROAD AND GENERAL AS THE CASING AIR: BUT NOW I AM CABINED, CRIBBED, CONFINED, BOUND IN TO SAUCY DOUBTS AND FEARS. —BUT BANQUO'S SAFE?

THANKS FOR THAT. THERE THE GROWN SERPENT LIES; THE WORM THAT'S FLED HATH NATURE THAT IN TIME WILL VENOM BREED, NO TEETH FOR THE PRESENT. GET THEE GONE. TOMORROW WE'LL HEAR OURSELVES AGAIN.

MY ROYAL LORD, YOU DO NOT GIVE THE CHEER. THE FEAST IS SOLD THAT IS NOT OFTEN VOUCHED, WHILE 'TIS A-MAKING, 'TIS GIVEN WITH WELCOME. TO FEED WERE BEST AT HOME; FROM THENCE, THE SAUCE TO MEAT IS CEREMONY; MEETING WERE BARE WITHOUT IT.

SWEET REMEMBRANCER! NOW GOOD DIGESTION WAIT ON APPETITE, AND HEALTH ON BOTH!

HERE HAD WE NOW OUR COUNTRY'S HONOUR ROOFED, WERE THE GRACED PERSON OF OUR BANQUO PRESENT; WHO MAY I RATHER CHALLENGE FOR UNKINDNESS THAN PITY FOR MISCHANCE.

MAY'T PLEASE YOUR HIGHNESS SIT.

HIS ABSENCE, SIR, LAYS BLAME UPON HIS PROMISE. PLEASE'T YOUR HIGHNESS TO GRACE US WITH YOUR ROYAL COMPANY?

THE TABLE'S FULL.

HERE IS A PLACE RESERVED, SIR.

WHERE?

HERE, MY GOOD LORD. WHAT IS'T THAT MOVES YOUR HIGHNESS?

WHICH OF YOU HAVE DONE THIS?

WHAT, MY GOOD LORD?

THOU CANST NOT SAY I DID IT:

NEVER SHAKE THY GORY LOCKS AT ME.

GENTLEMEN, RISE.
HIS HIGHNESS IS NOT WELL.

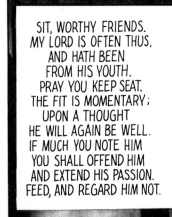

SIT, WORTHY FRIENDS.
MY LORD IS OFTEN THUS,
AND HATH BEEN
FROM HIS YOUTH.
PRAY YOU KEEP SEAT.
THE FIT IS MOMENTARY;
UPON A THOUGHT
HE WILL AGAIN BE WELL.
IF MUCH YOU NOTE HIM
YOU SHALL OFFEND HIM
AND EXTEND HIS PASSION.
FEED, AND REGARD HIM NOT.

ARE YOU A MAN?

AY, AND A BOLD ONE,
THAT DARE LOOK ON THAT
WHICH MIGHT APPAL THE DEVIL.

I DO FORGET.
DO NOT MUSE AT ME, MY MOST WORTHY FRIENDS:
I HAVE A STRANGE INFIRMITY, WHICH IS NOTHING
TO THOSE THAT KNOW ME. COME, LOVE AND HEALTH TO ALL;
THEN I'LL SIT DOWN. GIVE ME SOME WINE; FILL FULL!

I DRINK TO THE GENERAL JOY O'THE WHOLE TABLE,
AND TO OUR DEAR FRIEND BANQUO, WHOM WE MISS;
WOULD HE WERE HERE! TO ALL, AND HIM, WE THIRST,
AND ALL TO ALL!

OUR DUTIES, AND THE PLEDGE!

AVAUNT! AND QUIT MY SIGHT! LET THE EARTH HIDE
THEE! THY BONES ARE MARROWLESS, THY BLOOD IS
COLD; THOU HAST NO SPECULATION IN THOSE EYES
WHICH THOU DOST GLARE WITH.

THINK OF THIS, GOOD PEERS,
BUT AS A THING OF CUSTOM: 'TIS NO OTHER;
ONLY IT SPOILS THE PLEASURE OF THE TIME.

WHAT MAN DARE, I DARE.
APPROACH THOU LIKE THE RUGGED RUSSIAN BEAR,
THE ARMED RHINOCEROS, OR THE HYRCAN TIGER;
TAKE ANY SHAPE BUT THAT, AND MY FIRM NERVES
SHALL NEVER TREMBLE. OR BE ALIVE AGAIN,
AND DARE ME TO THE DESERT WITH THY SWORD;
IF TREMBLING I INHABIT THEN, PROTEST ME
THE BABY OF A GIRL. HENCE, HORRIBLE SHADOW!
UNREAL MOCKERY, HENCE!

WHY, SO; BEING GONE, I AM A MAN AGAIN.— PRAY YOU, SIT STILL.

YOU HAVE DISPLACED THE MIRTH, BROKE THE GOOD MEETING, WITH MOST ADMIRED DISORDER.

CAN SUCH THINGS BE, AND OVERCOME US LIKE A SUMMER'S CLOUD, WITHOUT OUR SPECIAL WONDER?

YOU MAKE ME STRANGE EVEN TO THE DISPOSITION THAT I OWE, WHEN NOW I THINK YOU CAN BEHOLD SUCH SIGHTS, AND KEEP THE NATURAL RUBY OF YOUR CHEEKS, WHEN MINE IS BLANCHED WITH FEAR.

WHAT SIGHTS, MY LORD?

I PRAY YOU, SPEAK NOT; HE GROWS WORSE AND WORSE; QUESTION ENRAGES HIM. AT ONCE, GOOD NIGHT. STAND NOT UPON THE ORDER OF YOUR GOING, BUT GO AT ONCE.

GOOD NIGHT; AND BETTER HEALTH ATTEND HIS MAJESTY!

A KIND GOOD NIGHT TO ALL!

IT WILL HAVE BLOOD, THEY SAY; BLOOD WILL HAVE BLOOD. STONES HAVE BEEN KNOWN TO MOVE AND TREES TO SPEAK; AUGURES AND UNDERSTOOD RELATIONS HAVE BY MAGGOT-PIES, AND CHOUGHS, AND ROOKS BROUGHT FORTH THE SECRET'ST MAN OF BLOOD. WHAT IS THE NIGHT?

ALMOST AT ODDS WITH MORNING, WHICH IS WHICH.

HOW SAYST THOU, THAT MACDUFF DENIES HIS PERSON AT OUR GREAT BIDDING?

DID YOU SEND TO HIM, SIR?

I HEAR IT BY THE WAY; BUT I WILL SEND. THERE'S NOT A ONE OF THEM, BUT IN HIS HOUSE I KEEP A SERVANT FEE'D. I WILL TOMORROW— AND BETIMES I WILL— TO THE WEIRD SISTERS: MORE SHALL THEY SPEAK; FOR NOW I AM BENT TO KNOW, BY THE WORST MEANS, THE WORST. FOR MINE OWN GOOD ALL CAUSES SHALL GIVE WAY. I AM IN BLOOD STEPPED IN SO FAR, THAT, SHOULD I WADE NO MORE, RETURNING WERE AS TEDIOUS AS GO O'ER. STRANGE THINGS I HAVE IN HEAD THAT WILL TO HAND, WHICH MUST BE ACTED ERE THEY MAY BE SCANNED.

YOU LACK THE SEASON OF ALL NATURES, SLEEP.

COME, WE'LL TO SLEEP. MY STRANGE AND SELF-ABUSE IS THE INITIATE FEAR THAT WANTS HARD USE. WE ARE YET BUT YOUNG IN DEED.

ACT III   SCENE V

WHY, HOW NOW, HECATE! YOU LOOK ANGERLY.

HAVE I NOT REASON, BELDAMS AS YOU ARE, SAUCY AND OVERBOLD? HOW DID YOU DARE TO TRADE AND TRAFFIC WITH MACBETH IN RIDDLES AND AFFAIRS OF DEATH; AND I, THE MISTRESS OF YOUR CHARMS, THE CLOSE CONTRIVER OF ALL HARMS, WAS NEVER CALLED TO BEAR MY PART, OR SHOW THE GLORY OF OUR ART? AND, WHICH IS WORSE, ALL YOU HAVE DONE HATH BEEN BUT FOR A WAYWARD SON, SPITEFUL AND WRATHFUL; WHO, AS OTHERS DO, LOVES FOR HIS OWN ENDS, NOT FOR YOU. BUT MAKE AMENDS NOW: GET YOU GONE, AND AT THE PIT OF ACHERON MEET ME IN THE MORNING: THITHER HE WILL COME TO KNOW HIS DESTINY. YOUR VESSELS AND YOUR SPELLS PROVIDE, YOUR CHARMS AND EVERYTHING BESIDE. I AM FOR THE AIR; THIS NIGHT I'LL SPEND UNTO A DISMAL AND A FATAL END: GREAT BUSINESS MUST BE WROUGHT ERE NOON: UPON THE CORNER OF THE MOON THERE HANGS A VAPOROUS DROP PROFOUND; I'LL CATCH IT ERE IT COME TO GROUND: AND THAT DISTILLED BY MAGIC SLEIGHTS SHALL RAISE SUCH ARTIFICIAL SPRITES AS BY THE STRENGTH OF THEIR ILLUSION SHALL DRAW HIM ON TO HIS CONFUSION. HE SHALL SPURN FATE, SCORN DEATH, AND BEAR HIS HOPES 'BOVE WISDOM, GRACE, AND FEAR: AND YOU ALL KNOW SECURITY IS MORTALS' CHIEFEST ENEMY.

HARK! I AM CALLED;

MY LITTLE SPIRIT, SEE, SITS IN A FOGGY CLOUD, AND STAYS FOR ME.

COME, LET'S MAKE HASTE; SHE'LL SOON BE BACK AGAIN.

MY FORMER SPEECHES HAVE
BUT HIT YOUR THOUGHTS,
WHICH CAN INTERPRET FURTHER.
ONLY I SAY THINGS HAVE
BEEN STRANGELY BORNE.

THE GRACIOUS DUNCAN
WAS PITIED OF MACBETH:
MARRY, HE WAS DEAD!
AND THE RIGHT VALIANT BANQUO
WALKED TOO LATE;
WHOM YOU MAY SAY,
IF'T PLEASE YOU,
FLEANCE KILLED,
FOR FLEANCE FLED.

MEN MUST NOT WALK TOO LATE.
WHO CANNOT WANT
THE THOUGHT HOW MONSTROUS
IT WAS FOR MALCOLM
AND FOR DONALBAIN
TO KILL THEIR GRACIOUS FATHER?
DAMNÈD FACT!
HOW IT DID GRIEVE
MACBETH!

DID HE NOT STRAIGHT,
IN PIOUS RAGE,
THE TWO DELINQUENTS TEAR,
THAT WERE THE SLAVES OF DRINK,
AND THRALLS OF SLEEP?
WAS NOT THAT NOBLY DONE?
AY,
AND WISELY TOO;

FOR 'TWOULD HAVE ANGERED
ANY HEART ALIVE
TO HEAR THE MEN DENY'T.
SO THAT, I SAY,
HE HAS BORNE ALL THINGS WELL:
AND I DO THINK THAT, HAD HE
DUNCAN'S SONS UNDER HIS KEY —
AS, AN'T PLEASE HEAVEN,
HE SHALL NOT —
THEY SHOULD FIND WHAT
'TWERE TO KILL A FATHER;
SO SHOULD FLEANCE.

BUT, PEACE!
FOR FROM BROAD
WORDS, AND 'CAUSE HE FAILED
HIS PRESENCE AT
THE TYRANT'S FEAST,
I HEAR MACDUFF LIVES IN DISGRACE.
SIR, CAN YOU TELL
WHERE HE BESTOWS HIMSELF?

THE SON OF DUNCAN, FROM WHOM THIS TYRANT HOLDS THE DUE OF BIRTH, LIVES IN THE ENGLISH COURT, AND IS RECEIVED OF THE MOST PIOUS EDWARD WITH SUCH GRACE THAT THE MALEVOLENCE OF FORTUNE NOTHING TAKES FROM HIS HIGH RESPECT.

THITHER MACDUFF IS GONE TO PRAY THE HOLY KING, UPON HIS AID TO WAKE NORTHUMBERLAND AND WARLIKE SIWARD; THAT BY THE HELP OF THESE— WITH HIM ABOVE TO RATIFY THE WORK— WE MAY AGAIN GIVE TO OUR TABLES MEAT, SLEEP TO OUR NIGHTS,

FREE FROM OUR FEASTS AND BANQUETS BLOODY KNIVES, DO FAITHFUL HOMAGE AND RECEIVE FREE HONOURS; ALL WHICH WE PINE FOR NOW. AND THIS REPORT HATH SO EXASPERATE THE KING THAT HE PREPARES FOR SOME ATTEMPT OF WAR.

SENT HE TO MACDUFF?

HE DID: AND WITH AN ABSOLUTE, 'SIR, NOT I', THE CLOUDY MESSENGER TURNS ME HIS BACK, AND HUMS, AS WHO SHOULD SAY, 'YOU'LL RUE THE TIME THAT CLOGS ME WITH THIS ANSWER.'

AND THAT WELL MIGHT ADVISE HIM TO A CAUTION, TO HOLD WHAT DISTANCE HIS WISDOM CAN PROVIDE.

SOME HOLY ANGEL FLY TO THE COURT OF ENGLAND AND UNFOLD HIS MESSAGE ERE HE COME, THAT A SWIFT BLESSING MAY SOON RETURN TO THIS OUR SUFFERING COUNTRY UNDER A HAND ACCURSED!

I'LL SEND MY PRAYERS WITH HIM!

THRICE THE BRINDED CAT HATH MEWED.

THRICE, AND ONCE THE HEDGE-PIG WHINED.

CRIES: 'TIS TIME, 'TIS TIME.

ROUND ABOUT THE CAULDRON GO; IN THE POISONED ENTRAILS THROW. TOAD, THAT UNDER COLD STONE DAYS AND NIGHTS HAS THIRTY-ONE. SWELTERED VENOM SLEEPING GOT, BOIL THOU FIRST I'THE CHARMED POT.

COOL IT WITH A BABOON'S BLOOD, THEN THE CHARM IS FIRM AND GOOD.

O! WELL DONE!
I COMMEND YOUR PAINS,
AND EVERYONE SHALL SHARE
I'THE GAINS:
AND NOW ABOUT THE CAULDRON SING,
LIKE ELVES AND FAIRIES IN A RING,
ENCHANTING ALL THAT YOU PUT IN.

BY THE PRICKING OF MY THUMBS, SOMETHING WICKED THIS WAY COMES. OPEN, LOCKS, WHOEVER KNOCKS!

HOW NOW, YOU SECRET, BLACK, AND MIDNIGHT HAGS! WHAT IS'T YOU DO?

A DEED WITHOUT A NAME.

I CONJURE YOU, BY THAT WHICH YOU PROFESS—HOWE'ER YOU COME TO KNOW IT—ANSWER ME:

THOUGH YOU UNTIE THE WINDS AND LET THEM FIGHT AGAINST THE CHURCHES; THOUGH THE YESTY WAVES CONFOUND AND SWALLOW NAVIGATION UP; THOUGH BLADED CORN BE LODGED AND TREES BLOWN DOWN; THOUGH CASTLES TOPPLE ON THEIR WARDERS' HEADS;

THOUGH PALACES AND PYRAMIDS DO SLOPE THEIR HEADS TO THEIR FOUNDATIONS; THOUGH THE TREASURE OF NATURE'S GERMENS TUMBLE ALL TOGETHER, EVEN TILL DESTRUCTION SICKEN; ANSWER ME TO WHAT I ASK YOU.

SPEAK.

DEMAND.

WE'LL ANSWER.

SAY IF THOU'DST RATHER HEAR IT FROM OUR MOUTHS, OR FROM OUR MASTERS?

CALL 'EM: LET ME SEE 'EM.

POUR IN SOW'S BLOOD THAT HATH EATEN HER NINE FARROW; GREASE THAT'S SWEATEN FROM THE MURDERER'S GIBBET, THROW INTO THE FLAME.

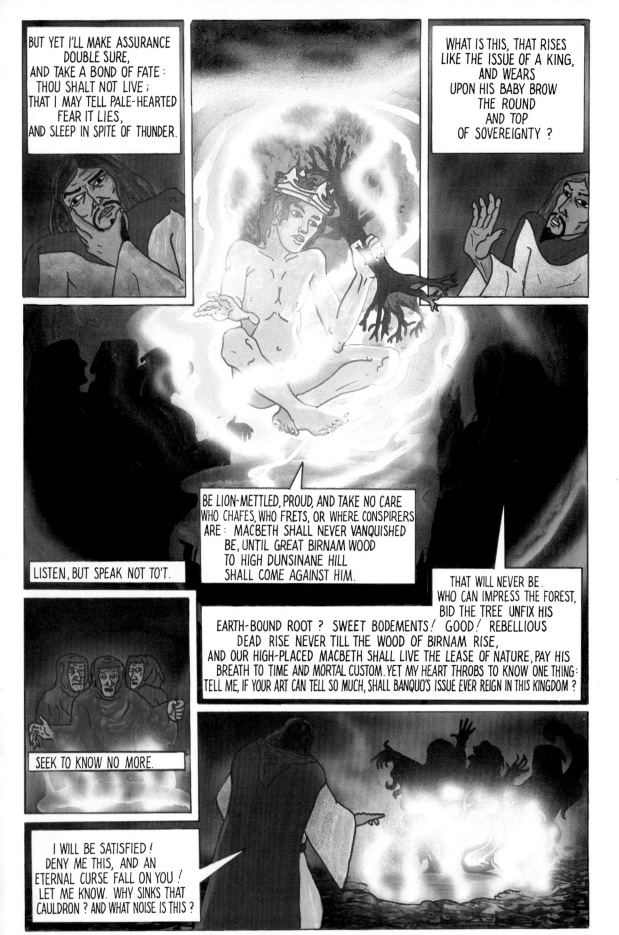

BUT YET I'LL MAKE ASSURANCE DOUBLE SURE, AND TAKE A BOND OF FATE: THOU SHALT NOT LIVE; THAT I MAY TELL PALE-HEARTED FEAR IT LIES, AND SLEEP IN SPITE OF THUNDER.

WHAT IS THIS, THAT RISES LIKE THE ISSUE OF A KING, AND WEARS UPON HIS BABY BROW THE ROUND AND TOP OF SOVEREIGNTY?

BE LION-METTLED, PROUD, AND TAKE NO CARE WHO CHAFES, WHO FRETS, OR WHERE CONSPIRERS ARE: MACBETH SHALL NEVER VANQUISHED BE, UNTIL GREAT BIRNAM WOOD TO HIGH DUNSINANE HILL SHALL COME AGAINST HIM.

LISTEN, BUT SPEAK NOT TO'T.

THAT WILL NEVER BE. WHO CAN IMPRESS THE FOREST, BID THE TREE UNFIX HIS EARTH-BOUND ROOT? SWEET BODEMENTS! GOOD! REBELLIOUS DEAD RISE NEVER TILL THE WOOD OF BIRNAM RISE, AND OUR HIGH-PLACED MACBETH SHALL LIVE THE LEASE OF NATURE, PAY HIS BREATH TO TIME AND MORTAL CUSTOM. YET MY HEART THROBS TO KNOW ONE THING: TELL ME, IF YOUR ART CAN TELL SO MUCH, SHALL BANQUO'S ISSUE EVER REIGN IN THIS KINGDOM?

SEEK TO KNOW NO MORE.

I WILL BE SATISFIED! DENY ME THIS, AND AN ETERNAL CURSE FALL ON YOU! LET ME KNOW. WHY SINKS THAT CAULDRON? AND WHAT NOISE IS THIS?

SHOW! SHOW! SHOW!

SHOW HIS EYES, AND GRIEVE HIS HEART; COME LIKE SHADOWS, SO DEPART.

THOU ART TOO LIKE THE SPIRIT OF BANQUO: DOWN!
THY CROWN DOES SEAR MINE EYEBALLS. AND THY HAIR, THOU OTHER GOLD-BOUND BROW, IS LIKE THE FIRST.
A THIRD IS LIKE THE FORMER. FILTHY HAGS! WHY DO YOU SHOW ME THIS? A FOURTH? START, EYES!
WHAT! WILL THE LINE STRETCH OUT TO THE CRACK OF DOOM? ANOTHER YET? A SEVENTH! I'LL SEE NO MORE:
AND YET THE EIGHTH APPEARS, WHO BEARS A GLASS WHICH SHOWS ME MANY MORE; AND SOME I SEE
THAT TWO-FOLD BALLS AND TREBLE SCEPTRES CARRY. HORRIBLE SIGHT! NOW I SEE 'TIS TRUE,
FOR THE BLOOD-BOLTERED BANQUO SMILES UPON ME, AND POINTS AT THEM FOR HIS. WHAT! IS THIS SO?

AY, SIR, ALL THIS IS SO. BUT WHY STANDS MACBETH THUS AMAZÈDLY? COME, SISTERS, CHEER WE UP HIS SPRITES, AND SHOW THE BEST OF OUR DELIGHTS. I'LL CHARM THE AIR TO GIVE A SOUND, WHILE YOU PERFORM YOUR ANTIC ROUND, THAT THIS GREAT KING MAY KINDLY SAY OUR DUTIES DID HIS WELCOME PAY.

WHERE ARE THEY ? GONE ?
LET THIS PERNICIOUS HOUR
STAND AYE ACCURSÈD IN THE CALENDAR.
COME IN, WITHOUT THERE !

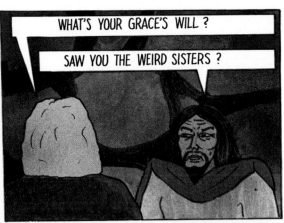

WHAT'S YOUR GRACE'S WILL ?

SAW YOU THE WEIRD SISTERS ?

NO, MY LORD.

CAME THEY NOT BY YOU ?

NO INDEED, MY LORD.

INFECTED BE THE AIR WHEREON THEY RIDE,
AND DAMNED ALL THOSE THAT TRUST THEM ! I DID HEAR
THE GALLOPING OF HORSE. WHO WAS'T CAME BY ?

'TIS TWO OR THREE, MY LORD,
THAT BRING YOU WORD.
MACDUFF IS FLED TO ENGLAND.

FLED TO ENGLAND !

AY, MY GOOD LORD.

TIME, THOU ANTICIPAT'ST MY DREAD EXPLOITS :
THE FLIGHTY PURPOSE NEVER IS O'ERTOOK
UNLESS THE DEED GO WITH IT. FROM THIS MOMENT
THE VERY FIRSTLINGS OF MY HEART SHALL BE
THE FIRSTLINGS OF MY HAND.
AND EVEN NOW, TO CROWN MY THOUGHTS WITH ACTS,
BE IT THOUGHT AND DONE :
THE CASTLE OF MACDUFF I WILL SURPRISE;
SEIZE UPON FIFE, GIVE TO THE EDGE O'THE SWORD
HIS WIFE, HIS BABES, AND ALL UNFORTUNATE SOULS
THAT TRACE HIM IN HIS LINE. NO BOASTING LIKE A FOOL;
THIS DEED I'LL DO BEFORE THIS PURPOSE COOL.
BUT NO MORE SIGHTS !
WHERE ARE THESE GENTLEMEN ?
COME, BRING ME WHERE THEY ARE.

ACT IV SCENE II

ENTER MACDUFF'S WIFE, HER SON, AND ROSS.

WHAT HAD HE DONE TO MAKE HIM FLY THE LAND?

YOU MUST HAVE PATIENCE, MADAM.

HE HAD NONE:
HIS FLIGHT WAS MADNESS: WHEN OUR ACTIONS DO NOT,
OUR FEARS DO MAKE US TRAITORS.

YOU KNOW NOT
WHETHER IT WAS HIS WISDOM OR HIS FEAR.

WISDOM! TO LEAVE HIS WIFE, TO LEAVE HIS BABES, HIS MANSION AND HIS TITLES, IN A PLACE FROM WHENCE HIMSELF DOES FLY? HE LOVES US NOT; HE WANTS THE NATURAL TOUCH: FOR THE POOR WREN,

THE MOST DIMINUTIVE OF BIRDS, WILL FIGHT, HER YOUNG ONES IN HER NEST, AGAINST THE OWL. ALL IS THE FEAR AND NOTHING IS THE LOVE; AS LITTLE IS THE WISDOM, WHERE THE FLIGHT SO RUNS AGAINST ALL REASON.

MY DEAREST CUZ,
I PRAY YOU, SCHOOL YOURSELF.
BUT, FOR YOUR HUSBAND, HE IS NOBLE, WISE, JUDICIOUS,
AND BEST KNOWS THE FITS O'THE SEASON.
I DARE NOT SPEAK MUCH FURTHER: BUT CRUEL ARE
THE TIMES, WHEN WE ARE TRAITORS AND DO NOT
KNOW OURSELVES; WHEN WE HOLD RUMOUR
FROM WHAT WE FEAR, YET KNOW NOT WHAT WE FEAR,
BUT FLOAT UPON A WILD AND VIOLENT SEA
EACH WAY AND MOVE. I TAKE MY LEAVE OF YOU:
SHALL NOT BE LONG BUT I'LL BE HERE AGAIN.
THINGS AT THE WORST WILL CEASE, OR ELSE CLIMB UPWARD
TO WHAT THEY WERE BEFORE.
MY PRETTY COUSIN, BLESSING UPON YOU!

FATHERED HE IS,
AND YET HE'S FATHERLESS.

I AM SO MUCH A FOOL, SHOULD I STAY LONGER
IT WOULD BE MY DISGRACE, AND YOUR DISCOMFORT.
I TAKE MY LEAVE AT ONCE.

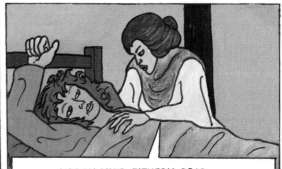

SIRRAH, YOUR FATHER'S DEAD:
AND WHAT WILL YOU DO NOW? HOW WILL YOU LIVE?

AS BIRDS DO, MOTHER.

WHAT, WITH WORMS AND FLIES?

WITH WHAT I GET, I MEAN;
AND SO DO THEY.

POOR BIRD! THOU'DST NEVER FEAR

THE NET NOR LIME,
THE PITFALL NOR THE GIN.

WHY SHOULD I, MOTHER?
POOR BIRDS THEY ARE NOT SET FOR.
MY FATHER IS NOT DEAD,
FOR ALL YOUR SAYING.

YES, HE IS DEAD:
HOW WILT THOU DO FOR A FATHER?

NAY, HOW WILL YOU
DO FOR A HUSBAND?

WHY, I CAN BUY ME TWENTY
AT ANY MARKET.

THEN YOU'LL BUY 'EM
TO SELL AGAIN.

THOU SPEAK'ST WITH ALL THY WIT;
AND YET, I'FAITH,
WITH WIT ENOUGH FOR THEE.

WAS MY FATHER A TRAITOR,
MOTHER?

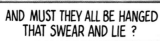

AY, THAT HE WAS.

WHAT IS A TRAITOR?

WHY, ONE THAT SWEARS AND LIES.

AND BE ALL TRAITORS THAT DO SO?

EVERYONE THAT DOES SO IS A TRAITOR,
AND MUST BE HANGED.

AND MUST THEY ALL BE HANGED
THAT SWEAR AND LIE?

EVERY ONE.

WHO MUST HANG THEM?

WHY, THE HONEST MEN.

THEN THE LIARS AND SWEARERS
ARE FOOLS;
FOR THERE ARE LIARS AND SWEARERS
ENOW TO BEAT THE HONEST MEN
AND HANG UP THEM.

IF HE WERE DEAD, YOU'D WEEP FOR HIM;
IF YOU WOULD NOT,
IT WERE A GOOD SIGN THAT I SHOULD
QUICKLY HAVE A NEW FATHER.

NOW GOD HELP THEE,
POOR MONKEY!
BUT HOW WILT THOU DO
FOR A FATHER?

POOR PRATTLER, HOW THOU TALK'ST!

BLESS YOU, FAIR DAME! I AM NOT TO YOU KNOWN,
THOUGH IN YOUR STATE OF HONOUR I AM PERFECT.
I DOUBT SOME DANGER DOES APPROACH YOU NEARLY.
IF YOU WILL TAKE A HOMELY MAN'S ADVICE,
BE NOT FOUND HERE; HENCE, WITH YOUR LITTLE ONES!
TO FIGHT YOU THUS, METHINKS I AM TOO SAVAGE;
TO DO WORSE TO YOU WERE FELL CRUELTY,
WHICH IS TOO NIGH YOUR PERSON. HEAVEN PRESERVE YOU!
I DARE ABIDE NO LONGER.

WHITHER SHOULD I FLY?
I HAVE DONE NO HARM. BUT I REMEMBER NOW
I AM IN THIS EARTHLY WORLD, WHERE TO DO
HARM IS OFTEN LAUDABLE, TO DO GOOD SOMETIME
ACCOUNTED DANGEROUS FOLLY. WHY THEN, ALAS!
DO I PUT UP THAT WOMANLY DEFENCE,
TO SAY I HAVE DONE NO HARM? —
WHAT ARE THESE FACES?

WHERE IS YOUR HUSBAND?

I HOPE IN NO PLACE SO UNSANCTIFIED
WHERE SUCH AS THOU MAYST FIND HIM.

HE'S A TRAITOR.

THOU LIEST, THOU SHAG-EARED VILLAIN!

WHAT! YOU EGG, YOUNG FRY OF TREACHERY!

HE HAS KILLED ME, MOTHER!
RUN AWAY, I PRAY YOU!

MURDER!!

65

ENTER MALCOLM AND MACDUFF

LET US SEEK OUT SOME DESOLATE SHADE, AND THERE WEEP OUR SAD BOSOMS EMPTY.

LET US RATHER HOLD FAST THE MORTAL SWORD, AND LIKE GOOD MEN BESTRIDE OUR DOWNFALL BIRTHDOM. EACH NEW MORN NEW WIDOWS HOWL, NEW ORPHANS CRY, NEW SORROWS STRIKE HEAVEN ON THE FACE, THAT IT RESOUNDS AS IF IT FELT WITH SCOTLAND AND YELLED OUT LIKE SYLLABLE OF DOLOUR.

WHAT I BELIEVE, I'LL WAIL; WHAT KNOW, BELIEVE, AND WHAT I CAN REDRESS, AS I SHALL FIND THE TIME TO FRIEND, I WILL. WHAT YOU HAVE SPOKE, IT MAY BE SO PERCHANCE. THIS TYRANT, WHOSE SOLE NAME BLISTERS OUR TONGUES, WAS ONCE THOUGHT HONEST: YOU HAVE LOVED HIM WELL; HE HATH NOT TOUCHED YOU YET. I AM YOUNG; BUT SOMETHING YOU MAY DESERVE OF HIM, THROUGH ME; AND WISDOM TO OFFER UP A WEAK, POOR, INNOCENT LAMB TO APPEASE AN ANGRY GOD.

I AM NOT TREACHEROUS.

BUT MACBETH IS.

A GOOD AND VIRTUOUS NATURE MAY RECOIL IN AN IMPERIAL CHARGE. BUT I SHALL CRAVE YOUR PARDON; THAT WHICH YOU ARE MY THOUGHTS CANNOT TRANSPOSE: ANGELS ARE BRIGHT STILL THOUGH THE BRIGHTEST FELL: THOUGH ALL THINGS FOUL WOULD WEAR THE BROWS OF GRACE, YET GRACE MUST STILL LOOK SO.

I HAVE LOST MY HOPES.

PERCHANCE EVEN THERE WHERE I DID FIND MY DOUBTS. WHY IN THAT RAWNESS LEFT YOU WIFE AND CHILD - THOSE PRECIOUS MOTIVES, THOSE STRONG KNOTS OF LOVE - WITHOUT LEAVE-TAKING? I PRAY YOU, LET NOT MY JEALOUSIES BE YOUR DISHONOURS, BUT MINE OWN SAFETIES: YOU MAY BE RIGHTLY JUST, WHATEVER I SHALL THINK.

BLEED, BLEED,
POOR COUNTRY!
GREAT TYRANNY,
LAY THOU THY BASIS SURE,
FOR GOODNESS DARE NOT CHECK THEE:
WEAR THOU THY WRONGS;
THE TITLE IS AFFEERED!
FARE THEE WELL, LORD:
I WOULD NOT BE THE VILLAIN
THAT THOU THINK'ST
FOR THE WHOLE SPACE
THAT'S IN THE TYRANT'S GRASP,
AND IN THE RICH
EAST TO BOOT.

BE NOT OFFENDED:
I SPEAK NOT AS IN ABSOLUTE FEAR OF YOU.
I THINK OUR COUNTRY SINKS BENEATH THE YOKE;
IT WEEPS, IT BLEEDS, AND EACH NEW DAY A GASH
IS ADDED TO HER WOUNDS. I THINK WITHAL,
THERE WOULD BE HANDS UPLIFTED IN MY RIGHT;
AND HERE FROM GRACIOUS ENGLAND HAVE I OFFER
OF GOODLY THOUSANDS. BUT FOR ALL THIS,
WHEN I SHALL TREAD UPON THE TYRANT'S HEAD,
OR WEAR IT UPON MY SWORD, YET MY POOR COUNTRY
SHALL HAVE MORE VICES THAN IT HAD BEFORE,
MORE SUFFER, AND MORE SUNDRY WAYS THAN EVER,
BY HIM THAT SHALL SUCCEED.

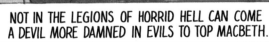

WHAT SHOULD HE BE?

IT IS MYSELF I MEAN; IN WHOM I KNOW
ALL THE PARTICULARS OF VICE SO GRAFTED
THAT, WHEN THEY SHALL BE OPENED, BLACK MACBETH
WILL SEEM AS PURE AS SNOW, AND THE POOR STATE
ESTEEM HIM AS A LAMB, BEING COMPARED
WITH MY CONFINELESS HARMS.

NOT IN THE LEGIONS OF HORRID HELL CAN COME
A DEVIL MORE DAMNED IN EVILS TO TOP MACBETH.

I GRANT HIM BLOODY,
LUXURIOUS, AVARICIOUS, FALSE, DECEITFUL,
SUDDEN, MALICIOUS, SMACKING OF EVERY SIN
THAT HAS A NAME: BUT THERE'S NO BOTTOM, NONE,
IN MY VOLUPTUOUSNESS. YOUR WIVES, YOUR DAUGHTERS,
YOUR MATRONS, AND YOUR MAIDS, COULD NOT FILL UP
THE CISTERN OF MY LUST; AND MY DESIRE
ALL CONTINENT IMPEDIMENTS WOULD O'ERBEAR
THAT DID OPPOSE MY WILL. BETTER MACBETH
THAN SUCH A ONE TO REIGN.

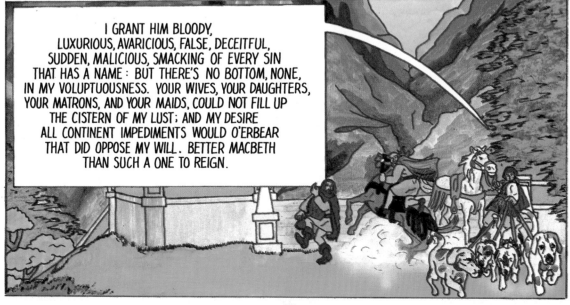

BOUNDLESS INTEMPERANCE
IN NATURE IS A TYRANNY; IT HATH BEEN
THE UNTIMELY EMPTYING OF THE HAPPY THRONE,
AND FALL OF MANY KINGS. BUT FEAR NOT YET
TO TAKE UPON YOU WHAT IS YOURS: YOU MAY
CONVEY YOUR PLEASURES IN A SPACIOUS PLENTY,
AND YET SEEM COLD, THE TIME YOU MAY SO HOODWINK.
WE HAVE WILLING DAMES ENOUGH; THERE CANNOT BE
THAT VULTURE IN YOU TO DEVOUR SO MANY
AS WILL TO GREATNESS DEDICATE THEMSELVES,
FINDING IT SO INCLINED.

WITH THIS THERE GROWS
IN MY MOST ILL-COMPOSED AFFECTION SUCH
A STAUNCHLESS AVARICE THAT, WERE I KING,
I SHOULD CUT OFF THE NOBLES FOR THEIR LANDS,
DESIRE HIS JEWELS AND THIS OTHER'S HOUSE;
AND MY MORE-HAVING WOULD BE AS A SAUCE
TO MAKE ME HUNGER MORE, THAT I SHOULD FORGE
QUARRELS UNJUST AGAINST THE GOOD AND LOYAL,
DESTROYING THEM FOR WEALTH.

THIS AVARICE
STICKS DEEPER, GROWS WITH MORE PERNICIOUS ROOT
THAN SUMMER-SEEMING LUST, AND IT HATH BEEN
THE SWORD OF OUR SLAIN KINGS. YET DO NOT FEAR;
SCOTLAND HATH FOISONS TO FILL UP YOUR WILL
OF YOUR MERE OWN. ALL THESE ARE PORTABLE,
WITH OTHER GRACES WEIGHED.

BUT I HAVE NONE.
THE KING-BECOMING GRACES,
AS JUSTICE, VERITY, TEMPERANCE, STABLENESS,
BOUNTY, PERSEVERANCE, MERCY, LOWLINESS,
DEVOTION, PATIENCE, COURAGE, FORTITUDE,
I HAVE NO RELISH OF THEM, BUT ABOUND
IN THE DIVISION OF EACH SEVERAL CRIME,
ACTING IT MANY WAYS. NAY, HAD I POWER, I SHOULD
POUR THE SWEET MILK OF CONCORD INTO HELL,
UPROAR THE UNIVERSAL PEACE, CONFOUND
ALL UNITY ON EARTH.

O SCOTLAND, SCOTLAND!

IF SUCH A ONE BE FIT TO GOVERN, SPEAK:
I AM AS I HAVE SPOKEN.

FIT TO GOVERN!
NO, NOT TO LIVE! O NATION MISERABLE,
WITH AN UNTITLED TYRANT, BLOODY-SCEPTRED,
WHEN SHALT THOU SEE THY WHOLESOME DAYS AGAIN,
SINCE THAT THE TRUEST ISSUE OF THY THRONE
BY HIS OWN INTERDICTION STANDS ACCUSED,
AND DOES BLASPHEME HIS BREED? THY ROYAL FATHER
WAS A MOST SAINTED KING; THE QUEEN THAT BORE THEE,
OFTENER UPON HER KNEES THAN ON HER FEET,
DIED EVERY DAY SHE LIVED. FARE THEE WELL!
THESE EVILS THOU REPEAT'ST UPON THYSELF
HATH BANISHED ME FROM SCOTLAND. O MY BREAST,
THY HOPE ENDS HERE!

MACDUFF, THIS NOBLE PASSION,
CHILD OF INTEGRITY, HATH FROM MY SOUL
WIPED THE BLACK SCRUPLES, RECONCILED MY THOUGHTS
TO THY GOOD TRUTH AND HONOUR. DEVILISH MACBETH
BY MANY OF THESE TRAINS HATH SOUGHT TO WIN ME
INTO HIS POWER, AND MODEST WISDOM PLUCKS ME
FROM OVER-CREDULOUS HASTE: BUT GOD ABOVE
DEAL BETWEEN THEE AND ME! FOR EVEN NOW
I PUT MYSELF TO THY DIRECTION, AND
UNSPEAK MINE OWN DETRACTION, HERE ABJURE
THE TAINTS AND BLAMES I LAID UPON MYSELF,
FOR STRANGERS TO MY NATURE.
I AM YET
UNKNOWN TO WOMAN, NEVER WAS FORSWORN,
SCARCELY HAVE COVETED WHAT WAS MINE OWN,
AT NO TIME BROKE MY FAITH, WOULD NOT BETRAY
THE DEVIL TO HIS FELLOW, AND DELIGHT
NO LESS IN TRUTH THAN LIFE. MY FIRST FALSE SPEAKING
WAS THIS UPON MYSELF. WHAT I AM TRULY
IS THINE AND MY POOR COUNTRY'S TO COMMAND;
WHITHER INDEED, BEFORE THY HERE-APPROACH,
OLD SIWARD WITH TEN THOUSAND WARLIKE MEN,
ALREADY AT A POINT, WAS SETTING FORTH.
NOW WE'LL TOGETHER, AND THE CHANCE OF GOODNESS
BE LIKE OUR WARRANTED QUARREL!
WHY ARE YOU SILENT?

SUCH WELCOME AND UNWELCOME THINGS
AT ONCE, 'TIS HARD TO RECONCILE.

WELL, MORE ANON.—
COMES THE KING FORTH, I PRAY YOU?

69

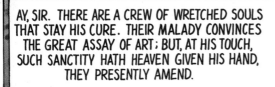

AY, SIR. THERE ARE A CREW OF WRETCHED SOULS THAT STAY HIS CURE. THEIR MALADY CONVINCES THE GREAT ASSAY OF ART; BUT, AT HIS TOUCH, SUCH SANCTITY HATH HEAVEN GIVEN HIS HAND, THEY PRESENTLY AMEND.

I THANK YOU, DOCTOR.

WHAT'S THE DISEASE HE MEANS?

'TIS CALLED THE EVIL: A MOST MIRACULOUS WORK IN THIS GOOD KING, WHICH OFTEN, SINCE MY HERE-REMAIN IN ENGLAND, I HAVE SEEN HIM DO. HOW HE SOLICITS HEAVEN HIMSELF BEST KNOWS: BUT STRANGELY-VISITED PEOPLE, ALL SWOLLEN AND ULCEROUS, PITIFUL TO THE EYE, THE MERE DESPAIR OF SURGERY, HE CURES; HANGING A GOLDEN STAMP ABOUT THEIR NECKS, PUT ON WITH HOLY PRAYERS; AND 'TIS SPOKEN, TO THE SUCCEEDING ROYALTY HE LEAVES THE HEALING BENEDICTION. WITH THIS STRANGE VIRTUE HE HATH A HEAVENLY GIFT OF PROPHECY, AND SUNDRY BLESSINGS HANG ABOUT HIS THRONE THAT SPEAK HIM FULL OF GRACE.

SEE, WHO COMES HERE?

MY COUNTRYMAN; BUT YET I KNOW HIM NOT.

MY EVER GENTLE COUSIN, WELCOME HITHER.

I KNOW HIM NOW. GOOD GOD, BETIMES REMOVE THE MEANS THAT MAKES US STRANGERS!

SIR, AMEN.

STANDS SCOTLAND WHERE IT DID?

ALAS, POOR COUNTRY, ALMOST AFRAID TO KNOW ITSELF! IT CANNOT BE CALLED OUR MOTHER, BUT OUR GRAVE; WHERE NOTHING, BUT WHO KNOWS NOTHING, IS ONCE SEEN TO SMILE; WHERE SIGHS AND GROANS AND SHRIEKS THAT RENT THE AIR ARE MADE, NOT MARKED; WHERE VIOLENT SORROW SEEMS A MODERN ECSTASY. THE DEAD MAN'S KNELL IS THERE SCARCE ASKED FOR WHO, AND GOOD MEN'S LIVES EXPIRE BEFORE THE FLOWERS IN THEIR CAPS, DYING OR ERE THEY SICKEN.

O, RELATION TOO NICE, AND YET TOO TRUE!

WHAT'S THE NEWEST GRIEF?

THAT OF AN HOUR'S AGE DOTH HISS THE SPEAKER; EACH MINUTE TEEMS A NEW ONE.

HOW DOES MY WIFE?

WHY, WELL.

AND ALL MY CHILDREN?

WELL TOO.

THE TYRANT HAS NOT BATTERED AT THEIR PEACE?

NO, THEY WERE WELL AT PEACE WHEN I DID LEAVE 'EM.

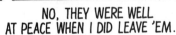

BE NOT A NIGGARD OF YOUR SPEECH: HOW GOES'T?

WHEN I CAME HITHER TO TRANSPORT THE TIDINGS WHICH I HAVE HEAVILY BORNE, THERE RAN A RUMOUR OF MANY WORTHY FELLOWS THAT WERE OUT; WHICH WAS TO MY BELIEF WITNESSED THE RATHER FOR THAT I SAW THE TYRANT'S POWER AFOOT. NOW IS THE TIME OF HELP. YOUR EYE IN SCOTLAND WOULD CREATE SOLDIERS, MAKE OUR WOMEN FIGHT, TO DOFF THEIR DIRE DISTRESSES.

BE'T THEIR COMFORT, WE ARE COMING THITHER. GRACIOUS ENGLAND HATH LENT US GOOD SIWARD AND TEN THOUSAND MEN; AN OLDER AND BETTER SOLDIER NONE THAT CHRISTENDOM GIVES OUT.

WOULD I COULD ANSWER THIS COMFORT WITH THE LIKE! BUT I HAVE WORDS THAT WOULD BE HOWLED OUT IN THE DESERT AIR, WHERE HEARING SHOULD NOT LATCH THEM.

WHAT CONCERN THEY? THE GENERAL CAUSE? OR IS IT A FEE-GRIEF DUE TO SOME SINGLE BREAST?

NO MIND THAT'S HONEST BUT IN IT SHARES SOME WOE, THOUGH THE MAIN PART PERTAINS TO YOU ALONE.

LET NOT YOUR EARS DESPISE MY TONGUE FOR EVER, WHICH SHALL POSSESS THEM WITH THE HEAVIEST SOUND THAT EVER YET THEY HEARD.

IF IT BE MINE, KEEP IT NOT FROM ME; QUICKLY LET ME HAVE IT.

HUMH! I GUESS AT IT.

YOUR CASTLE IS SURPRISED; YOUR WIFE AND BABES SAVAGELY SLAUGHTERED. TO RELATE THE MANNER, WERE, ON THE QUARRY OF THESE MURDERED DEER, TO ADD THE DEATH OF YOU.

MERCIFUL HEAVEN!

WHAT, MAN! NE'ER PULL YOUR HAT UPON YOUR BROWS. GIVE SORROW WORDS: THE GRIEF THAT DOES NOT SPEAK WHISPERS THE O'ER-FRAUGHT HEART AND BIDS IT BREAK.

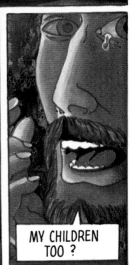

MY CHILDREN TOO?

WIFE, CHILDREN, SERVANTS, ALL THAT COULD BE FOUND.

AND I MUST BE FROM THENCE! MY WIFE KILLED TOO?

BE COMFORTED: LET'S MAKE US MED'CINES OF OUR GREAT REVENGE, TO CURE THIS DEADLY GRIEF.

I HAVE SAID.

HE HAS NO CHILDREN.
ALL MY PRETTY ONES? DID YOU SAY ALL?
O HELL-KITE! ALL? WHAT, ALL MY PRETTY CHICKENS
AND THEIR DAM AT ONE FELL SWOOP?

DISPUTE IT LIKE A MAN.

I SHALL DO SO;
BUT I MUST ALSO FEEL IT AS A MAN.
I CANNOT BUT REMEMBER SUCH THINGS WERE,
THAT WERE MOST PRECIOUS TO ME. DID HEAVEN LOOK ON
AND WOULD NOT TAKE THEIR PART? SINFUL MACDUFF,
THEY WERE ALL STRUCK FOR THEE! NAUGHT THAT I AM,
NOT FOR THEIR OWN DEMERITS, BUT FOR MINE,
FELL SLAUGHTER ON THEIR SOULS. HEAVEN REST THEM NOW.

BE THIS THE WHETSTONE OF YOUR SWORD: LET GRIEF
CONVERT TO ANGER; BLUNT NOT THE HEART, ENRAGE IT.

O, I COULD PLAY THE WOMAN WITH MINE EYES,
AND BRAGGART WITH MY TONGUE. BUT, GENTLE HEAVENS,
CUT SHORT ALL INTERMISSION; FRONT TO FRONT
BRING THOU THIS FIEND OF SCOTLAND AND MYSELF;
WITHIN MY SWORD'S LENGTH SET HIM;
IF HE 'SCAPE, HEAVEN FORGIVE HIM TOO!

THIS TUNE GOES MANLY.
COME, GO WE TO THE KING; OUR POWER IS READY;
OUR LACK IS NOTHING BUT OUR LEAVE. MACBETH
IS RIPE FOR SHAKING, AND THE POWERS ABOVE
PUT ON THEIR INSTRUMENTS. RECEIVE WHAT CHEER
YOU MAY: THE NIGHT IS LONG THAT NEVER FINDS THE DAY.

ACT V SCENE 1

I HAVE TWO NIGHTS WATCHED WITH YOU, BUT CAN PERCEIVE NO TRUTH IN YOUR REPORT. WHEN WAS IT SHE LAST WALKED?

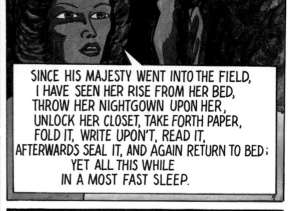

SINCE HIS MAJESTY WENT INTO THE FIELD, I HAVE SEEN HER RISE FROM HER BED, THROW HER NIGHTGOWN UPON HER, UNLOCK HER CLOSET, TAKE FORTH PAPER, FOLD IT, WRITE UPON'T, READ IT, AFTERWARDS SEAL IT, AND AGAIN RETURN TO BED; YET ALL THIS WHILE IN A MOST FAST SLEEP.

A GREAT PERTURBATION IN NATURE, TO RECEIVE AT ONCE THE BENEFIT OF SLEEP AND DO THE EFFECTS OF WATCHING! IN THIS SLUMBERY AGITATION, BESIDES HER WALKING AND OTHER ACTUAL PERFORMANCES WHAT, AT ANY TIME, HAVE YOU HEARD HER SAY?

THAT, SIR, WHICH I WILL NOT REPORT AFTER HER.

YOU MAY TO ME, AND 'TIS MOST MEET YOU SHOULD.

NEITHER TO YOU NOR ANYONE, HAVING NO WITNESS TO CONFIRM MY SPEECH.

LO YOU! HERE SHE COMES. THIS IS HER VERY GUISE; AND, UPON MY LIFE, FAST ASLEEP. OBSERVE HER; STAND CLOSE.

HOW CAME SHE BY THAT LIGHT?

YOU SEE HER EYES ARE OPEN.

WHY, IT STOOD BY HER: SHE HAS LIGHT BY HER CONTINUALLY; 'TIS HER COMMAND.

AY, BUT THEIR SENSE ARE SHUT.

WHAT IS IT SHE DOES NOW?
LOOK, HOW SHE RUBS HER HANDS.

IT IS AN ACCUSTOMED ACTION WITH HER,
TO SEEM THUS WASHING HER HANDS.
I HAVE KNOWN HER CONTINUE IN THIS
A QUARTER OF AN HOUR.

YET HERE'S A SPOT.

HARK! SHE SPEAKS.
I WILL SET DOWN WHAT COMES FROM HER, TO
SATISFY MY REMEMBRANCE THE MORE STRONGLY.

OUT, DAMNED SPOT! OUT, I SAY!
ONE: TWO: WHY, THEN 'TIS TIME TO DO'T.
HELL IS MURKY! FIE, MY LORD, FIE!
A SOLDIER, AND AFEARD?
WHAT NEED WE FEAR WHO KNOWS IT,
WHEN NONE CAN CALL OUR POWER TO ACCOMPT?
YET WHO WOULD HAVE THOUGHT THE OLD MAN
TO HAVE HAD SO MUCH BLOOD IN HIM?

DO YOU MARK THAT?

THE THANE OF FIFE HAD A WIFE; WHERE IS SHE NOW?
WHAT! WILL THESE HANDS NE'ER BE CLEAN?
NO MORE O'THAT, MY LORD, NO MORE O'THAT:
YOU MAR ALL WITH THIS STARTING.

GO TO, GO TO; YOU HAVE KNOWN WHAT YOU SHOULD NOT.

SHE HAS SPOKE WHAT SHE SHOULD NOT, I AM SURE OF THAT: HEAVEN KNOWS WHAT SHE HAS KNOWN.

HERE'S THE SMELL OF THE BLOOD STILL: ALL THE PERFUMES OF ARABIA WILL NOT SWEETEN THIS LITTLE HAND. OH! OH! OH!

WHAT A SIGH IS THERE! THE HEART IS SORELY CHARGED.

I WOULD NOT HAVE SUCH A HEART IN MY BOSOM FOR THE DIGNITY OF THE WHOLE BODY.

WELL, WELL, WELL,—

PRAY GOD IT BE, SIR.

THIS DISEASE IS BEYOND MY PRACTICE; YET I HAVE KNOWN THOSE WHICH HAVE WALKED IN THEIR SLEEP WHO HAVE DIED HOLILY IN THEIR BEDS.

WASH YOUR HANDS, PUT ON YOUR NIGHT-GOWN; LOOK NOT SO PALE! I TELL YOU YET AGAIN, BANQUO'S BURIED; HE CANNOT COME OUT ON'S GRAVE.

EVEN SO?

TO BED, TO BED! THERE'S KNOCKING AT THE GATE. COME, COME, COME, COME, GIVE ME YOUR HAND. WHAT'S DONE CANNOT BE UNDONE. TO BED, TO BED, TO BED.

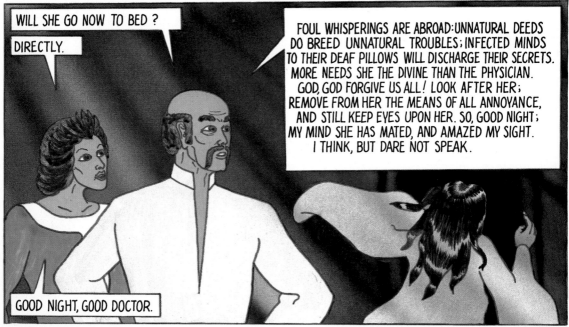

WILL SHE GO NOW TO BED?

DIRECTLY.

FOUL WHISPERINGS ARE ABROAD: UNNATURAL DEEDS DO BREED UNNATURAL TROUBLES; INFECTED MINDS TO THEIR DEAF PILLOWS WILL DISCHARGE THEIR SECRETS. MORE NEEDS SHE THE DIVINE THAN THE PHYSICIAN. GOD, GOD FORGIVE US ALL! LOOK AFTER HER; REMOVE FROM HER THE MEANS OF ALL ANNOYANCE, AND STILL KEEP EYES UPON HER. SO, GOOD NIGHT; MY MIND SHE HAS MATED, AND AMAZED MY SIGHT. I THINK, BUT DARE NOT SPEAK.

GOOD NIGHT, GOOD DOCTOR.

THE ENGLISH POWER IS NEAR, LED ON BY MALCOLM, HIS UNCLE SIWARD, AND THE GOOD MACDUFF. REVENGES BURN IN THEM; FOR THEIR DEAR CAUSES WOULD TO THE BLEEDING AND THE GRIM ALARM EXCITE THE MORTIFIED MAN.

NEAR BIRNAM WOOD SHALL WE WELL MEET THEM; THAT WAY ARE THEY COMING.

WHO KNOWS IF DONALBAIN BE WITH HIS BROTHER?

FOR CERTAIN, SIR, HE IS NOT. I HAVE A FILE OF ALL THE GENTRY: THERE IS SIWARD'S SON, AND MANY UNROUGH YOUTHS THAT EVEN NOW PROTEST THEIR FIRST OF MANHOOD.

WHAT DOES THE TYRANT?

GREAT DUNSINANE HE STRONGLY FORTIFIES. SOME SAY HE'S MAD; OTHERS, THAT LESSER HATE HIM, DO CALL IT VALIANT FURY: BUT, FOR CERTAIN, HE CANNOT BUCKLE HIS DISTEMPERED CAUSE WITHIN THE BELT OF RULE.

NOW DOES HE FEEL
HIS SECRET MURDERS STICKING ON HIS HANDS;
NOW MINUTELY REVOLTS UPBRAID HIS FAITH-BREACH.
THOSE HE COMMANDS MOVE ONLY IN COMMAND,
NOTHING IN LOVE. NOW DOES HE FEEL HIS TITLE
HANG LOOSE ABOUT HIM, LIKE A GIANT'S ROBE
UPON A DWARFISH THIEF.

WHO THEN SHALL BLAME HIS
PESTERED SENSES TO RECOIL AND START,
WHEN ALL THAT IS WITHIN HIM DOES CONDEMN
ITSELF FOR BEING THERE?

WELL, MARCH WE ON
TO GIVE OBEDIENCE WHERE 'TIS TRULY OWED:
MEET WE THE MED'CINE OF THE SICKLY WEAL,
AND WITH HIM POUR WE, IN OUR COUNTRY'S PURGE,
EACH DROP OF US.

OR SO MUCH AS IT NEEDS
TO DEW THE SOVEREIGN FLOWER AND DROWN THE WEEDS.
MAKE WE OUR MARCH TOWARDS BIRNAM.

ACT V   SCENE III

THE DEVIL DAMN THEE BLACK, THOU CREAM-FACED LOON! WHERE GOT'ST THOU THAT GOOSE LOOK?

BRING ME NO MORE REPORTS; LET THEM FLY ALL!
TILL BIRNAM WOOD REMOVE TO DUNSINANE
I CANNOT TAINT WITH FEAR. WHAT'S THE BOY MALCOLM?
WAS HE NOT BORN OF WOMAN? THE SPIRITS THAT KNOW
ALL MORTAL CONSEQUENCES HAVE PRONOUNCED ME THUS:
'FEAR NOT, MACBETH; NO MAN THAT'S BORN OF WOMAN
SHALL E'ER HAVE POWER UPON THEE.' THEN FLY,
FALSE THANES, AND MINGLE WITH THE ENGLISH EPICURES:
THE MIND I SWAY BY AND THE HEART I BEAR
SHALL NEVER SAG WITH DOUBT NOR SHAKE WITH FEAR.

THERE IS TEN THOUSAND—

GEESE, VILLAIN?

SOLDIERS, SIR.

GO PRICK THY FACE AND OVER-RED THY FEAR,
THOU LILY-LIVERED BOY. WHAT SOLDIERS, PATCH?
DEATH OF THY SOUL! THOSE LINEN CHEEKS OF THINE
ARE COUNSELLORS TO FEAR. WHAT SOLDIERS, WHEY-FACE?

THE ENGLISH FORCE, SO PLEASE YOU.

TAKE THY FACE HENCE.

SEYTON!— I AM SICK AT HEART
WHEN I BEHOLD— SEYTON, I SAY!— THIS PUSH
WILL CHAIR ME EVER OR DIS-SEAT ME NOW.
I HAVE LIVED LONG ENOUGH: MY WAY OF LIFE
IS FALLEN INTO THE SERE, THE YELLOW LEAF;
AND THAT WHICH SHOULD ACCOMPANY OLD AGE,
AS HONOUR, LOVE, OBEDIENCE, TROOPS OF FRIENDS,
I MUST NOT LOOK TO HAVE; BUT IN THEIR STEAD,
CURSES, NOT LOUD, BUT DEEP, MOUTH-HONOUR, BREATH
WHICH THE POOR HEART WOULD FAIN DENY AND DARE NOT.
SEYTON!

WHAT'S YOUR GRACIOUS PLEASURE?

WHAT NEWS MORE?

ALL IS CONFIRMED, MY LORD,
WHICH WAS REPORTED.

I'LL FIGHT TILL FROM MY BONES MY FLESH BE HACKED.
GIVE ME MY ARMOUR.

'TIS NOT NEEDED YET.

I'LL PUT IT ON.
SEND OUT MORE HORSES, SKIRR THE COUNTRY ROUND,
HANG THOSE THAT TALK OF FEAR. GIVE ME MINE ARMOUR.
HOW DOES YOUR PATIENT, DOCTOR?

NOT SO SICK, MY LORD,
AS SHE IS TROUBLED WITH THICK-COMING FANCIES,
THAT KEEP HER FROM HER REST.

CURE HER OF THAT:
CANST THOU NOT MINISTER TO A MIND DISEASED,
PLUCK FROM THE MEMORY A ROOTED SORROW,
RAZE OUT THE WRITTEN TROUBLES OF THE BRAIN,
AND WITH SOME SWEET OBLIVIOUS ANTIDOTE
CLEANSE THE STUFFED BOSOM OF THAT PERILOUS STUFF
WHICH WEIGHS UPON THE HEART?

THEREIN THE PATIENT MUST MINISTER TO HIMSELF.

THROW PHYSIC TO THE DOGS, I'LL NONE OF IT!
COME, PUT MINE ARMOUR ON; GIVE ME MY STAFF.
SEYTON, SEND OUT.— DOCTOR, THE THANES FLY FROM ME.—
COME, SIR, DISPATCH.— IF THOU COULDST, DOCTOR, CAST
THE WATER OF MY LAND, FIND HER DISEASE,
AND PURGE IT TO A SOUND AND PRISTINE HEALTH,
I WOULD APPLAUD THEE TO THE VERY ECHO,
THAT SHOULD APPLAUD AGAIN.— PULL'T OFF, I SAY.—
WHAT RHUBARB, SENNA, OR WHAT PURGATIVE DRUG
WOULD SCOUR THESE ENGLISH HENCE? HEAR'ST THOU OF THEM?

AY, MY GOOD LORD; YOUR ROYAL PREPARATION
MAKES US HEAR SOMETHING.

BRING IT AFTER ME.
I WILL NOT BE AFRAID OF DEATH AND BANE
TILL BIRNAM FOREST COME TO DUNSINANE.

WERE I FROM DUNSINANE AWAY AND CLEAR,
PROFIT AGAIN SHOULD HARDLY DRAW ME HERE.

ACT V SCENE IV

WHAT WOOD IS THIS BEFORE US?

COUSINS,
I HOPE THE DAYS ARE NEAR AT HAND
THAT CHAMBERS WILL BE SAFE.

WE DOUBT IT NOTHING.

THE WOOD OF BIRNAM.

LET EVERY SOLDIER HEW HIM DOWN A BOUGH
AND BEAR'T BEFORE HIM; THEREBY SHALL WE SHADOW
THE NUMBERS OF OUR HOST, AND MAKE DISCOVERY
ERR IN REPORT OF US.

IT SHALL BE DONE.

WE LEARN NO OTHER BUT THE CONFIDENT TYRANT
KEEPS STILL IN DUNSINANE, AND WILL ENDURE
OUR SETTING DOWN BEFORE'T.

'TIS HIS MAIN HOPE:
FOR WHERE THERE IS ADVANTAGE TO BE GIVEN,
BOTH MORE AND LESS HAVE GIVEN HIM THE REVOLT,
AND NONE SERVE WITH HIM BUT CONSTRAINED THINGS
WHOSE HEARTS ARE ABSENT TOO.

LET OUR JUST CENSURES
ATTEND THE TRUE EVENT, AND PUT WE ON
INDUSTRIOUS SOLDIERSHIP.

THE TIME APPROACHES
THAT WILL WITH DUE DECISION MAKE US KNOW
WHAT WE SHALL SAY WE HAVE AND WHAT WE OWE.
THOUGHTS SPECULATIVE THEIR UNSURE HOPES RELATE,
BUT CERTAIN ISSUE STROKES MUST ARBITRATE;
TOWARDS WHICH ADVANCE THE WAR.

HANG OUT OUR BANNERS ON THE OUTWARD WALLS;
THE CRY IS STILL, 'THEY COME': OUR CASTLE'S STRENGTH
WILL LAUGH A SIEGE TO SCORN: HERE LET THEM LIE
TILL FAMINE AND THE AGUE EAT THEM UP.
WERE THEY NOT FORCED WITH THOSE THAT SHOULD BE OURS,
WE MIGHT HAVE MET THEM DAREFUL, BEARD TO BEARD,
AND BEAT THEM BACKWARD HOME.

WHAT IS THAT NOISE?

IT IS THE CRY OF WOMEN,
MY GOOD LORD.

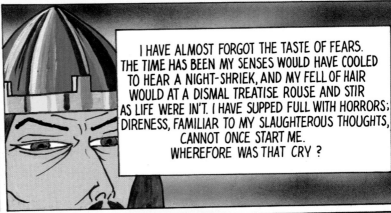

I HAVE ALMOST FORGOT THE TASTE OF FEARS.
THE TIME HAS BEEN MY SENSES WOULD HAVE COOLED
TO HEAR A NIGHT-SHRIEK, AND MY FELL OF HAIR
WOULD AT A DISMAL TREATISE ROUSE AND STIR
AS LIFE WERE IN'T. I HAVE SUPPED FULL WITH HORRORS;
DIRENESS, FAMILIAR TO MY SLAUGHTEROUS THOUGHTS,
CANNOT ONCE START ME.
WHEREFORE WAS THAT CRY?

THE QUEEN, MY LORD, IS DEAD.

SHE SHOULD HAVE DIED HEREAFTER;
THERE WOULD HAVE BEEN A TIME FOR SUCH A WORD.
TOMORROW, AND TOMORROW, AND TOMORROW,
CREEPS IN THIS PETTY PACE FROM DAY TO DAY,
TO THE LAST SYLLABLE OF RECORDED TIME;
AND ALL OUR YESTERDAYS HAVE LIGHTED FOOLS
THE WAY TO DUSTY DEATH. OUT, OUT, BRIEF CANDLE!
LIFE'S BUT A WALKING SHADOW, A POOR PLAYER
THAT STRUTS AND FRETS HIS HOUR UPON THE STAGE,
AND THEN IS HEARD NO MORE. IT IS A TALE
TOLD BY AN IDIOT, FULL OF SOUND AND FURY,
SIGNIFYING NOTHING.

THOU COM'ST TO USE THY
TONGUE; THY STORY QUICKLY!

GRACIOUS MY LORD,
I SHOULD REPORT THAT WHICH I SAY I SAW,
BUT KNOW NOT HOW TO DO IT.

WELL, SAY, SIR.

AS I DID STAND MY WATCH UPON THE HILL,
I LOOKED TOWARD BIRNAM, AND ANON METHOUGHT
THE WOOD BEGAN TO MOVE.

LIAR AND SLAVE!

LET ME ENDURE YOUR WRATH IF'T BE NOT SO:
WITHIN THIS THREE MILE MAY YOU SEE IT COMING.
I SAY, A MOVING GROVE.

IF THOU SPEAK'ST FALSE,
UPON THE NEXT TREE SHALL THOU HANG ALIVE,
TILL FAMINE CLING THEE.

IF THY SPEECH BE SOOTH,
I CARE NOT IF THOU DOST FOR ME AS MUCH.
I PULL IN RESOLUTION, AND BEGIN TO DOUBT
THE EQUIVOCATION OF THE FIEND THAT LIES LIKE TRUTH:
'FEAR NOT, TILL BIRNAM WOOD DO COME TO DUNSINANE'—
AND NOW A WOOD COMES TOWARD DUNSINANE.
ARM, ARM, AND OUT!
IF THIS WHICH HE AVOUCHES DOES APPEAR,
THERE IS NOR FLYING HENCE, NOR TARRYING HERE.
I 'GIN TO BE AWEARY OF THE SUN,
AND WISH THE ESTATE O'THE WORLD WERE NOW UNDONE.
RING THE ALARUM BELL! BLOW, WIND! COME, WRACK!
AT LEAST WE'LL DIE WITH HARNESS ON OUR BACK.

ACT V SCENE VII

THEY HAVE TIED ME TO A STAKE; I CANNOT FLY,
BUT BEAR-LIKE I MUST FIGHT THE COURSE.
WHAT'S HE THAT WAS NOT BORN OF WOMAN?
SUCH A ONE AM I TO FEAR, OR NONE.

WHAT IS THY NAME?

THOU'LT BE AFRAID TO HEAR IT.

NO; THOUGH THOU CALL'ST THYSELF
A HOTTER NAME THAN ANY IS IN HELL.

MY NAME'S MACBETH.

THE DEVIL HIMSELF COULD NOT PRONOUNCE
A TITLE MORE HATEFUL TO MINE EAR.

NO, NOR MORE FEARFUL.

THOU LIEST, ABHORRÈD TYRANT! WITH MY SWORD
I'LL PROVE THE LIE THOU SPEAK'ST.

THOU WAST BORN OF WOMAN.
BUT SWORDS I SMILE AT, WEAPONS LAUGH TO SCORN,
BRANDISHED BY MAN THAT'S OF A WOMAN BORN.

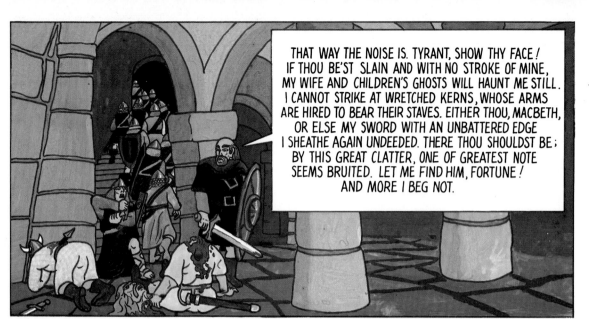

THAT WAY THE NOISE IS. TYRANT, SHOW THY FACE!
IF THOU BE'ST SLAIN AND WITH NO STROKE OF MINE,
MY WIFE AND CHILDREN'S GHOSTS WILL HAUNT ME STILL.
I CANNOT STRIKE AT WRETCHED KERNS, WHOSE ARMS
ARE HIRED TO BEAR THEIR STAVES. EITHER THOU, MACBETH,
OR ELSE MY SWORD WITH AN UNBATTERED EDGE
I SHEATHE AGAIN UNDEEDED. THERE THOU SHOULDST BE;
BY THIS GREAT CLATTER, ONE OF GREATEST NOTE
SEEMS BRUITED. LET ME FIND HIM, FORTUNE!
AND MORE I BEG NOT.

THIS WAY, MY LORD; THE CASTLE'S GENTLY RENDERED;
THE TYRANT'S PEOPLE ON BOTH SIDES DO FIGHT;
THE NOBLE THANES DO BRAVELY IN THE WAR;
THE DAY ALMOST ITSELF PROFESSES YOURS,
AND LITTLE IS TO DO.

WE HAVE MET WITH FOES THAT STRIKE BESIDE US.

ENTER, SIR, THE CASTLE.

WHY SHOULD I PLAY THE ROMAN FOOL, AND DIE ON MINE OWN SWORD? WHILES I SEE LIVES, THE GASHES DO BETTER UPON THEM.

TURN, HELL-HOUND, TURN!

OF ALL MEN ELSE I HAVE AVOIDED THEE. BUT GET THEE BACK! MY SOUL IS TOO MUCH CHARGED WITH BLOOD OF THINE ALREADY.

I HAVE NO WORDS; MY VOICE IS IN MY SWORD, THOU BLOODIER VILLAIN THAN TERMS CAN GIVE THEE OUT!

THOU LOSEST LABOUR: AS EASY MAYEST THOU THE INTRENCHANT AIR WITH THY KEEN SWORD IMPRESS AS MAKE ME BLEED: LET FALL THY BLADE ON VULNERABLE CRESTS; I BEAR A CHARMÈD LIFE, WHICH MUST NOT YIELD TO ONE OF WOMAN BORN.

DESPAIR THY CHARM, AND LET THE ANGEL WHOM THOU STILL HAST SERVED TELL THEE, MACDUFF WAS FROM HIS MOTHER'S WOMB UNTIMELY RIPPED.

ACCURSÈD BE THAT TONGUE THAT TELLS ME SO, FOR IT HATH COWED MY BETTER PART OF MAN: AND BE THESE JUGGLING FIENDS NO MORE BELIEVED, THAT PALTER WITH US IN A DOUBLE SENSE, THAT KEEP THE WORD OF PROMISE TO OUR EAR, AND BREAK IT TO OUR HOPE. I'LL NOT FIGHT WITH THEE.

THEN YIELD THEE, COWARD, AND LIVE TO BE THE SHOW AND GAZE O'THE TIME. WE'LL HAVE THEE, AS OUR RARER MONSTERS ARE, PAINTED UPON A POLE, AND UNDERWRIT, 'HERE MAY YOU SEE THE TYRANT.'

I WILL NOT YIELD
TO KISS THE GROUND BEFORE YOUNG MALCOLM'S FEET,
AND TO BE BAITED WITH THE RABBLE'S CURSE.
THOUGH BIRNAM WOOD BE COME TO DUNSINANE,
AND THOU OPPOSED, BEING OF NO WOMAN BORN,
YET I WILL TRY THE LAST.
BEFORE MY BODY I THROW MY WARLIKE SHIELD.
LAY ON, MACDUFF,
AND DAMNED BE HIM THAT FIRST CRIES,
'HOLD, ENOUGH !'

I WOULD THE FRIENDS WE MISS WERE SAFE ARRIVED.

SOME MUST GO OFF; AND YET, BY THESE I SEE, SO GREAT A DAY AS THIS IS CHEAPLY BOUGHT.

MACDUFF IS MISSING, AND YOUR NOBLE SON.

YOUR SON, MY LORD, HAS PAID A SOLDIER'S DEBT: HE ONLY LIVED BUT TILL HE WAS A MAN; THE WHICH NO SOONER HAD HIS PROWESS CONFIRMED IN THE UNSHRINKING STATION WHERE HE FOUGHT, BUT LIKE A MAN HE DIED.

THEN HE IS DEAD?

AY, AND BROUGHT OFF THE FIELD. YOUR CAUSE OF SORROW MUST NOT BE MEASURED BY HIS WORTH, FOR THEN IT HATH NO END.

HAD HE HIS HURTS BEFORE?

AY, ON THE FRONT.

WHY THEN, GOD'S SOLDIER BE HE! HAD I AS MANY SONS AS I HAVE HAIRS, I WOULD NOT WISH THEM TO A FAIRER DEATH: AND SO HIS KNELL IS KNOLLED.

HE'S WORTH MORE SORROW, AND THAT I'LL SPEND FOR HIM.

HE'S WORTH NO MORE: THEY SAY HE PARTED WELL, AND PAID HIS SCORE: AND SO GOD BE WITH HIM! —HERE COMES NEWER COMFORT.

HAIL, KING! FOR SO THOU ART. BEHOLD, WHERE STANDS
THE USURPER'S CURSÈD HEAD. THE TIME IS FREE.
I SEE THEE COMPASSED WITH THY KINGDOM'S PEARL,
THAT SPEAK MY SALUTATION IN THEIR MINDS,
WHOSE VOICES I DESIRE ALOUD WITH MINE.
HAIL, KING OF SCOTLAND!